# THE LIFE OF THE RENOWNED SR PHILIP SIDNEY (1652)

## By Fulke Greville

**A FACSIMILE REPRODUCTION WITH AN INTRODUCTION BY WARREN W. WOODEN**

**SCHOLARS' FACSIMILES & REPRINTS
DELMAR, NEW YORK, 1984**

SCHOLARS' FACSIMILES & REPRINTS
ISSN 0161-2279
SERIES ESTABLISHED 1936
VOLUME 390

Published by
Scholars' Facsimiles & Reprints
Delmar, New York 12054

**Library of Congress Cataloging in Publication Data**

Greville, Fulke, Baron Brooke, 1554-1628.
The life of the renowned Sr. Philip Sidney.

1. Sidney, Philip, Sir, 1554-1586—Biography.
2. Authors, English—Early modern, 1500-1700—Biography.
I. Title.
PR2343.B7    1983    821'.3    [B]    83-4483
ISBN 0-8201-1390-5

# INTRODUCTION

## Biographical Context

"FVLKE GREVILL, SERVANT TO QVEENE ELIZABETH, CON-
CELLER TO KING JAMES, AND FREND TO SIR PHILIP SIDNEY.
TROPHAEVM PECCATI." Inscribed on the tomb in Warwick that
Greville designed for himself after abandoning plans to build a tomb
in St. Paul's in London to hold both his body and Sidney's, this
epitaph attests to the central role Philip Sidney occupied in Fulke
Greville's mind. Sidney was first a school mate and friend, then an
inspiration, and finally, in the years after his premature death when
Greville's nostalgia perfected his memory, a peerless pattern for
emulation. According to the autobiographical chapter 14 of the
*Life of Sidney*, Greville set out to emulate his friend in both the
active and contemplative spheres. As he outlived his youth, however, Greville came to realize his own and the time's incapacity
for matching Sidney's gifts. Thus, as a memorial to him, Greville
wrote a "dedication" which survives today as the *Life Of the Renowned Sr Philip Sidney.*

Greville was uniquely qualified to write such a work. He first
met Sidney in 1564 when their fathers enrolled the boys, then
both ten years of age, in the Shrewsbury grammar school. Their
friendship ripened four years until they went separate ways for
their university education, Greville to Cambridge and Sidney to
Oxford. In 1575 their friendship resumed when Sidney's father introduced them both to court; the following decade, until Sidney's
departure for the Netherlands in 1585, is the period of their mature friendship. The two went abroad together on Sidney's em-
bassy of condolence to Emperor Rudolph II in 1577, and then again
in 1582 as part of the company escorting the Duc d'Anjou to the
Low Countries, and they planned to sail with Drake on an expedition to the New World in 1584. As members of the court party
led by Sidney's uncle, the Earl of Leicester, the two young men
shared a commitment to the ideals of the anti-Spanish, activist

Protestant circle at court, both were eager for diplomatic or military foreign service for the crown, and both took an interest in the literary ferment and experimentation of the period. In sum, Greville knew Sidney as well as any man can know another, sharing his hopes and disappointments, his aspirations and accomlishments.

Despite his devotion to Sidney and the powerful sense of loss Greville records in his correspondence following his friend's death, this event did not move Greville immediately to begin a biography to memorialize his friend. Greville did write a verse elegy on Sidney, printed in a collection of such pieces in 1595, but there is no indication that he contemplated a biography of Sidney during the sixteenth century. For literature was no more Greville's vocation than it had been Sidney's; both men saw themselves as courtiers trained for careers in active service to the state. Although Greville wrote some sonnets during the 1570s and 1580s, apparently in friendly rivalry with Sidney, his larger literary projects all date from a later time.[1] Instead, Greville sought advancement through public service, winning a seat in Parliament from Warwickshire in 1586 and receiving the award of the offices of clerk of the council in the Marches of Wales in 1590. In 1598 Greville was appointed treasurer of the Navy, and his status as trusted counsellor to Queen Elizabeth enabled him to ride out the fall of the Earl of Essex, his patron and leader of his party at court.

With the death of Elizabeth, however, Greville's fortunes changed abruptly. His greatest political opponent, Robert Cecil, secured a grip on power as the new monarch's chief minister. The following year, 1604, Greville was forced out of his post with the Navy and began a decade of retirement at Warwick Castle which did not end until the death of Cecil in 1614 reopened the possibility of further public service. It was during this period of self-imposed exile in Warwickshire that Greville worked on closet-dramas, begun apparently in the late 1590s, and wrote and revised his *Life of Sidney.* At the death of Cecil, Greville returned to London and resumed his public career, which led ultimately to his appointment as Chancellor of the Exchequer in 1621. During the period of his service under the Stuarts, until his death in 1628 at the hands of a disgruntled servant, Greville wrote his verse treatises on war, human learning, and religion.[2]

Several features are worth observing about the biographical context from which the *Life of Sidney* emerged. Although Greville possessed ample materials to have written an intimate, anecdotal biography of his friend, this was not his purpose in the *Life*. The work contains reminiscences which every reader prizes, such as Greville's and Sidney's doubtful dealings with Francis Drake, but Greville was primarily interested less in drawing a portrait of Sidney the individual, a complex of hopes and fears, strengths and weaknesses, than of Sidney the Christian patriot, an exemplum of moral and civic virtue. One of Greville's most recent biographers describes the *Life* as a "political hagiography";[3] while the label is too narrow, it is true that Greville is less interested in portraying Sidney the individual than Sidney the model public servant and embodiment of the genius of the Elizabethan era. Greville's approach to the story of Sidney's life was conditioned both by the Renaissance conception of life-writing, which ultimately goes back to Plutarch's *Lives of the Noble Grecians and Romans,* and by his personal situation. During the sixteenth century in England, life-writing was considered to be a frankly partisan undertaking in which one praised or damned his subject, always being careful, as in Thomas More's *History of Richard III* or William Roper's *Life of More,* to set forth the subject as a moral exemplum of either virtue or vice. Meanwhile, on a personal basis, Greville seems always to have deferred to the quick wit and abundant talent of his friend, whose gifts Greville knew he could not match. When he came to write the story of his friend's life as an introductory treatise to stand before a collection of Greville's own plays, the tendency to aggrandize the comrade of his youth must have been irresistible. Greville had first begun his literary career in friendly competition with Sidney in the 1570s; now, in a different century and under a different monarch, he set out to write an account of his friend to preface a collection of his literary endeavors, "these exercises of my youth."[4] Exiled and aged, for in his fifties Greville was old by the standards of his time, Greville saw Sidney as the antithesis of the grasping, corrupt, self-serving courtiers who dominated the court of James, and in Greville's hands, Sidney's portrait became a "seamark" for all the virtuous to steer by and a stinging rebuke to a corrupt age.

In brief, the exemplary nature of the *Life of Sidney* is fundamental to both its shape and content. Greville wrote it so that "our nation may see a Sea-mark, rais'd upon their native coast, above the levell of any private Pharos abroad: and so by a right Meridian line of their own, learn to sayl through the straits of true vertue, into a calm, and spacious Ocean of humane honour" (p. 4). It should also be noted that Greville did not rely simply on his personal reminiscences of Sidney; the *Life* is more than a memoir. He researched those areas of Sidney's life and career which required special emphasis in the portrait he wanted to paint. Thus, although Greville did not accompany Sidney on his final expedition to the Low Countries and so was not with him at his death, as Joan Rees observes, "there is, in fact, more detail in Greville's account of the weeks when Sidney lay dying than there is for any other period in Sidney's life and the details are far from indiscriminate."[5] Just as Greville selected key events throughout Sidney's life for emphasis in his account, so he patterned the incidents surrounding the death to bring out the qualities of courage, morality, and magnanimity which make Sidney's death as exemplary as his life. The *Life*, then, is a portrait of Sidney, a testimonial to an extraordinary friendship, an exemplary pattern of moral and civic virtue, and a rebuke to a degenerate society which had abandoned Sidney's values.

## Date and Text

One of the chief problems, perhaps an insoluble one, in dealing with the Greville canon is the difficulty of establishing the composition dates and final texts of his works. Although Greville apparently considered publication of his works from time to time (and it is to one such time that we owe the *Life of Sidney*), for a variety of personal and professional reasons he decided against this course. Instead, Greville kept his works by him, revising and polishing them, putting scribes to work to copy out various recensions. This habit of "perpetual revision," as one critic calls it,[6] has important consequences for the *Life of Sidney* just as it does for Greville's other work.

The present work was published twenty-four years after Greville's death by one "P.B.," who is responsible for both the cumbrous title of the work and the dedication to Lady Dorothea Sidney. The manuscript from which the anonymous publisher set up the 1652 edition is lost, but in the nineteenth century an early manuscript version of the work was discovered in the library of Trinity College, Cambridge. This is a good copy of the *Life* bearing the title "A Dedication to Sr Philip Sidney," containing a number of mostly minor variants which can be used to correct readings in the 1652 edition. The Cambridge manuscript and the printed edition of 1652 obviously descend from a common lost ancestor; Nowell Smith, whose edition of 1907 attempted to collate the two versions, declines to speculate on "which version has the better claim to represent the author's *summa manus.*"[7] Then, in the early 1950s, another seventeenth-century manuscript of the *Life* was discovered in the Shrewsbury Public Library, a manuscript significantly different from either of the two other versions. As described by S. Blaine Ewing, the Shrewsbury manuscript of the *Life* is over 5,000 words shorter than its fellows, and it rearranges some of the material it shares with the others.[8] The bulk of the material not in the Shrewsbury manuscript deals with Queen Elizabeth and her policies, including almost all of chapter 9 in the printed edition.[9] Prominent among the omissions in the Shrewsbury version is Greville's account (see pp. 242-50) of his plan to write a history of the Tudors and, in particular, a life of Queen Elizabeth until he was blocked by Robert Cecil's refusal to give him access to the state papers from her reign.

Despite the difficulties of dating either of the two manuscript copies of the *Life*,[10] Greville scholars seem pretty well agreed on the thesis that the Shrewsbury manuscript represents the earlier version of the *Life* and that in the Cambridge manuscript and the printed text of 1652 we have a later revised version into which Greville inserted much of the material he had gathered for a biography of Elizabeth before he was thwarted by Cecil.[11] While there is some disagreement over whether Greville had completed his tinkering with the *Life*, this dispute is largely academic. And just as there is a consensus on the order of the versions, so there is on their approximate date of composition: 1609-14. Presumably Greville laid aside the work, and his plans to publish it, when he resumed his public career in 1614; certainly the criticism of King James's policies, always implicit and occasionally explicit in Greville's paean to Queen Elizabeth in the latter chapters of the *Life*, would not have furthered the author's public ambitions.

## Themes

The 1652 edition of the *Life* contains three distinct sections which suggest the major thematic concerns of the work. Chapters 1-13 constitute a biography of Sidney, a pattern of moral and civic virtue; chapters 15-17 focus on Queen Elizabeth and the wisdom of her policies; and chapters 14 and 18 discuss Greville's art, his intent in his plays, and his aesthetic. While there is some overlapping among these three divisions, they do serve to indicate the major themes of the *Life* which, as Charles A. Larson illustrates, are moral, political, and aesthetic.[12] As moral tract, the *Life* is frequently described as "hagiographic," the life of a courtier-soldier as Protestant saint.[13] From this perspective, the *Life* may be seen to borrow precepts not from the *Golden Legend* but from such secular treatises as Castiglione's *Book of the Courtier* and to illustrate them in action in the life of a Protestant hero. Sidney is "a true modell of Worth" (p. 38) for all citizens, for "that his heart and tongue went both one way, and so with every one that went with the Truth" (p. 41). In each sphere of activity Greville considers in the *Life,* Sidney is guided by his concern first for the morality and second for the advancement of his country. ("Neither was this in him a private, but a publique affection; his chief ends being not Friends, Wife, Children, or himself; but above all things the honour of his Maker, and service of his Prince, or Country" [p. 47].) Thus in each area of Sidney's career which Greville elects to discuss— Sidney as author, diplomatic strategist, military leader, etc.—the moral underpinnings and goal of each activity are carefully explicated. Not surprisingly, in the process, all negative features, if Greville were ever aware of any in Sidney, are expunged from the portrait to view Sidney consistently as a type and pattern. As Joan Rees observes, however, the *Life* is saved from becoming a panegyric to abstract virtue because "although the enlivening personal detail is usually absent, yet the whole is firmly rooted in Greville's memory of particulars, of times, places, and individuals."[14] Nevertheless, the moral intent and exemplary function of the *Life* are paramount and consistent, dominating all other aspects of the work.

Politically, the *Life* represents a brief for what is described by historians as the "radical Protestant" program of the Elizabethan faction centered about the Earl of Leicester and, later, the Earl of Essex. The hallmark of this program, according to Ronald Rebholz, was "their insistence that religion should determine national policy."[15] Thus, throughout the *Life,* Greville argues for an activist foreign policy which would see English military might and diplomatic support extended to the Protestant states of Europe in pursuit of a grand Protestant alliance against the global designs for conquest and control by Spain and the Roman Catholic church. Greville attributes to Sidney a key role in the codification of this policy, and it is clear throughout the *Life* that not only Greville but a number of important figures, in England and on the continent, saw Sidney as the vigorous and committed leader who could one day translate this political program into reality. With Sidney's death and, later, the fall of Essex, whose essential loyalty and ideals Greville warmly defends in the *Life*, the more moderate policies of limited entanglement with foreign alliances and reduced engagements against Spanish power advocated by the Cecils increasingly guided Elizabethan foreign policy. Finally, with the passing of the Queen, a new monarch with little taste for war or hostility toward Spain and the preeminence of Robert Cecil in his council turned the government away from the policies of the radical Protestants so decisively that Greville himself was forced out of office.

During this period of exclusion from public service when he retired to Warwick Castle to think, write, and wait, the age of Elizabeth, epitomized by his brilliant friend Sidney who symbolized for Greville all that was best in that age, came to stand in stark relief as a reproach to the conciliatory policy and pervasive corruption of the Jacobean regime. Thus, to the exaltation of Sidney and his age contained in the Shrewsbury manuscript of the *Life*, Greville returned some time after Cecil's refusal to grant him access to the state papers for his projected biography of Elizabeth and added the new material on Elizabeth's foreign and domestic policies to the *Life*. This material is so developed that the reader is repeatedly encouraged to contrast Elizabeth's policies and method of government to those of her successor, who is never explicitly named in these comparisons. However, when Greville discusses Elizabeth's means of holding her favorites and ministers in check, guarding against excess or abuse while listening respectfully to and acting upon advice from her counselors and parliaments, the contrast with James could not have escaped seventeenth-century readers.[16] Thus, as the bulky title of the printed edition suggests, a strong topical political theme recurs throughout the *Life*.

Greville's comments on the nature and value of literature, which arise from his consideration of both Sidney's literary efforts and his own, constitute a third major concern in the *Life*. Although this theme is likely to be of keenest interest to many modern readers, it receives less emphasis from Greville than either of the other two major concerns. This is a natural circumstance, since Greville did not consider either himself or his friend primarily as authors but perceived both as active leaders in the life of the country. Thus Greville's failure to mention Sidney's *Apology for Poetry* or *Astro-*

*phel and Stella* is not surprising; indeed, if Greville had decided upon an in-depth survey of Sidney's verse, given the kind of biography he was writing, he would surely have emphasized the translations of the Psalms and religious lyrics. Greville does consider at some length the *Arcadia*, in whose publication he had had a hand, and his thrust here is to see the romance as of a piece with the rest of Sidney's life—as another moral exemplum, in Greville's terms. In addition to teaching the lessons of good governance through the fictional narrative of *Arcadia*, Greville declares that "(I know) his purpose was to limn out such exact pictures, of every posture in the minde, that any man being forced, in the straines of this life, to pass through any straights, or latitudes of good, or ill fortune, might (as in a glasse) see how to set a good countenance upon all the discountenances of adversitie, and a stay upon the exorbitant smiling of chance" (pp. 18-19). Greville goes on to recount that as he matured, Sidney's concerns, including his literary ones, became more serious and sober, prompting him, after the familiar Vergilian precedent, to bequeath "no other legacie, but the fire, to this unpolished Embrio" (pp. 19-20). It has often been pointed out that this attitude sounds more like Greville than Sidney, and in his discussion of his own imaginative productions, Greville makes a famous comparison of his own literary endeavors with Sidney's:

> For my own part, I found my creeping Genius more fixed upon the Images of Life, than the Images of Wit, and therefore chose not to write to them on whose foot the black Oxe had not already trod, as the Proverbe is, but to those only, that are weather-beaten in the Sea of this World, such as having lost the sight of their Gardens, and groves, study to saile on a right course among Rocks, and quicksands; And . . . in this ordaining, and ordering matter, and forme together for the use of life, I have made those Tragedies, no Plaies for the Stage. . . (pp. 253-54).

Greville's literary efforts were of a different order from those of his friend, of a more sober and pessimistic cast, productions designed to aid the reader's passage through a world whose contours seemed far bleaker to Greville than they had to the young Sidney.

### Design and Artistry

The most serious and the most common charge leveled against the *Life of Sidney*, a charge echoed even by its admirers, is that the work lacks coherent, artistic design. Thus, it is not a real biography at all but a "rambling tribute" (Donald A. Stauffer), a work in which the author has "thrown aside formal rules of literary composition" (Morris Croll), so that it "spreads out, in the unchanneled abundance of our earlier prose and the retiring soliloquizing of Greville's older age, into a 'Treatise,' in which the primary object is clean forgotten" (Nowell Smith).[17] In sum, because of its disorganized rambling and lack of focus, the critics see the *Life* as "a feeble biographical effort" (Paul M. Kendall), "marred by a lack of control in conception and structure, with the consequence that a certain formlessness becomes one of its most noticeable characteristics" (Charles Larson).[18]

In fact, however, the *Life of Sidney* is based on a clear, traditional design which would have been apparent to many of its original readers. Greville's biography takes as its formal model the classical demonstrative oration devised by the rhetoricians of ancient Greece and Rome to confer praise, or occasionally blame, upon a person. The principles, or topics, of such encomiastic orations were commonplaces in the Elizabethan educational curriculum, and Greville would have been acquainted with them from both his grammar school and university studies. The rhetoricians offered a skeletal outline for arranging and assigning weight to the various features of a subject's life for analysis and praise; and, while offering a firm outline, the sequence was also flexible enough to be adapted to various subjects—indeed, Sidney even adapted it to praise not a person but a thing, Poetry, in his *Apology for Poetry.*[19]

As described by Greville's acquaintance, Dr. Thomas Wilson, in his popular text *The Arte of Rhetorique* (1553; rev. ed., 1560), the author of such an oration should proceed chronologically in his survey of the subject's life with special emphasis on "The tyme of his departure, or death."[20] Within this chronological framework, special topics are to be emphasized. In the subject's youth, for example, "for bringing vp of a noble personage, his nurse must bee considered, his play fellowes observed, his teacher and his seruants called in remembraunces."[21] Upon his arrival at manhood, his "inclination of nature" should be examined, along with testimonies to his character from those who knew him. These opening topics of the demonstrative oration as described by Wilson provide a blueprint for the first three chapters of Greville's *Life,* where he describes the esteemed continental humanist Hubert Languet, who as Sidney's friend and unofficial tutor functioned as "a Nurse of knowledge to this hopefull young Gentleman" (p. 8), while Greville himself provides first-hand evidence of Sidney's bearing as a schoolboy, and the testimony of both the English and continental notables witnesses to the high moral character and boundless potential of young Sidney. The analysis of *Arcadia* as a moral tract in chapter 2 is similarly part of an assessment of the young Sidney's "inclination of nature." The remainder of Greville's biography, that is, the first thirteen chapters of the *Life,* follows the topoi of the demonstrative oration through the discussion of "attempts worthie," domestic and foreign (chapters 4-7); "His pollicies and wittie deuices, in behoufe of the publique weale" (chapters 8-10); and finally, a detailed analysis of "Things that haue happened about his death" (chapters 11-13).

In fact, then, the first thirteen chapters of the *Life of Sidney* follow without significant deviation the classical schemata of the demonstrative oration. Reference to this model also explains the apparent "digressions" cited by critics of the work. The two most extensive departures from the chronological narrative are the testimonials and analysis of Sidney's character in chapters 2-3 and the so-called "map of Europe" survey of European geopolitics in chapters 8-10; the first of these corresponds to Wilson's heading of the subject's "inclination of nature" and the second answers to his call for evidence of the subject's "wise counsaile." This latter section is lengthened because Sidney's life in the public, active sphere was largely one of potential rather than achievement, and to bring out the full greatness of Sidney, extra stress was required on his invaluable advice and plans for action. Thus, the supposed curiosities of Greville's narrative may be explained by reference to this model, the demonstrative oration, and his adaptation of its schemata to the particular circumstances of his subject's life.

Greville's rhetorical design is most clear in the earlier version of the *Life* preserved in the Shrewsbury manuscript. When he revised the work to incorporate the materials he had gathered toward a biography of Queen Elizabeth, Greville was confronted with the problem of artistic unity and coherence. The addition of the material on Elizabeth and her policies inevitably obscured his original design; almost all of chapter 9, part of the "map of Europe" section of the biography, was introduced at this point into the original design represented by the Shrewsbury version. To compensate for the blurring of narrative unity, Greville attempted to emphasize the thematic unity between portions of the work. To meld the new material with the old into a unit, Greville sharpened and reasserted the thematic role of the key individuals portrayed in his narrative.

Sidney, of course, remained the focus as "a Sea-mark, rais'd upon their native coast" (p. 4) to show the English how a citizen could order his private and public lives so as to maintain his integrity and contribute to his country even in the most trying circumstances. Queen Elizabeth was likewise described with the same figure as "a Sea-mark to warn all Creatures under her that shee had still a creating, or defacing power inherent in her Crown and Person, above those subalterne places by which shee did minister universall justice" (p. 207). Through its implicit comment on her successor's policies, the new material on Elizabeth, which came into the Cambridge manuscript and 1652 printed text, enlarged and pointed how Elizabeth served as the pattern of a godly governor to complement the portrait of Sidney as a godly citizen. These are the two central portraits in the narrative, of Sidney and his queen, two exemplary individuals who stood above the flux, confusion, and corruption of their times to see clearly and act rightly for the advancement of God and country.

These two major portraits in the foreground of the *Life* are raised into high relief by the subsidiary portraits of figures in Greville's narrative. To adopt Greville's own metaphor, most men struggle to stay afloat without compromising their principles upon the treacherous seas of life. Because of their God-given gifts and natural superiority, some few rise like Sidney and Elizabeth above the waters to guide and inspire those navigating the seas of life. Of those caught in the tide, two individuals receive special scrutiny from Greville. There is, first, Greville himself, always conscious of taking second place, of deferring to Sidney. Despite his service to Elizabeth, Greville was not allowed the military or diplomatic career he hungered for and, in the ripeness of his age, he was cast aside, a victim of court politics, to write somber treatises for those who had felt the impress of the black ox's hoof. Yet Greville neither begrudges his brilliant friend his fame nor blames the queen who thwarted his ambitions of foreign service; on the contrary, whether describing his relations with either person or speaking directly to their qualities, Greville is uniformly laudatory. Hence, the reader confronts throughout in Greville's reminiscences and reflections an authorial persona who details his own efforts to steer a course true to the values of these beacons whose radiance he celebrates.

Like Greville's portrait of himself, another figure viewed as a good man trying to navigate the shoals and hidden reefs of public life is Robert Devereux, Earl of Essex. In Essex's case, examined in chapter 14, the Earl's passage was cut short due to his own errors of judgment and the inveterate hatred of his enemies at court. Greville advances a warm defense of his kinsman in the *Life,* excusing his intent, although not his actions, and arguing Essex's innocence of the treason charge: "So that his heart bee (as in my conscience it was) free from this unnaturall crime, yet these *unreturning* steps seemed well worth the observing" (pp. 181-82). Greville's own difficulties in surviving amidst the intrigue of partisan politics are yoked with those of Essex: "This sudden descent of such greatnesse, together with the quality of the Actors in every Scene, stir'd up the Authors second thoughts, to bee carefull (in his owne case) of leaving faire weather behind him" (p. 179). Indeed, even the metaphor of sailing treacherous seas is carried over: "My selfe, his Kinsman, and while I remained about the *Queen,* a kinde of *Remora,* staying the violent course of that fatall Ship, and these winde-watching Passengers (at least, as his enemies imagined) abruptly sent away to guard a figurative Fleet, in danger of nothing but these *Prosopopeia's* of invisible rancor. . . . " (pp. 180-81). Thus, down in the flood from which the beacons of Sidney and Elizabeth arise, good men of the caliber of Greville and Essex struggle against the tide. These portraits fill in a background which adds luster to the achievements of Sidney and Elizabeth and reinforces the pervasive view in the *Life* of this world as a treacherous and unstable resting place.

Other minor portraits assist in clarifying Greville's vision of the world and reinforcing his themes. The portrait of Elizabeth, the wise monarch, comments implicitly throughout on a portrait underlying Greville's text, that of James I, the inept monarch. Also serving an antithetical function is the portrait of the Earl of Oxford, whose behavior toward Sidney in the tennis court contretemps affords a clear contrast between the proud, egotistical, and self-serving courtier and the good courtier. This portrait of Oxford also occurs in a context which provides a good illustration of Greville's management of narrative incident. The tennis court affair is a self-contained episode carefully crafted and moralized by Greville to illustrate the theme of Sidney's sense of honor, duty, and self.

The controlling metaphor for the tennis court affair is dramatic; the incident wears the trappings of tragedy, although through a *deus ex machina* (in this case, Queen Elizabeth), it turns into a bloodless triumph for Sidney. Oxford, the antagonist, is first introduced, and Greville rapidly traces the rising tension as the Earl encounters young Sidney on the tennis court and orders him off. Greville summarizes this initial exchange between Oxford and Sidney, moving from summary to a close paraphrase of Sidney's reply which reproduces the antithesis of the original: "Sir *Philip* temperately answers; that if his Lordship had been pleased to express desire in milder Characters, perchance he should have led out those, that he should now find would not be driven out with any scourge of fury" (p. 76). Oxford's abusive retort of "Puppy" is given verbatim, along with the audience reaction of the attentive French commissioners in the upper gallery. A brief exchange between the two men elicits Sidney's final reply, giving Oxford "a Lie, impossible . . . to be retorted," which Greville quotes in full: "all the world knows, Puppies are gotten by Dogs, and Children by men" (p. 77). Having set the stage and audience and brought the principal players together for a dramatic exchange. Greville prolongs the tension: "both stood silent a while, like a dumb shew in a Tragedy" (*ibid.*). Abruptly, Sidney quits the playing court and retires to await the formal challenge from Oxford which should follow. As Sidney waits and Oxford procrastinates, however, the Queen initiates a counter-move to resolve by fiat the threat of tragedy in her court. At this juncture, Greville brings together his two heroes, Sidney and Queen Elizabeth, for a consult which provides a rhetorical climax to this mini-drama. The Queen speaks magisterially of degree and duty; Sidney responds, "with such reverence as became him," setting forth the traditional rights and principles of Englishmen to freedom from the caprice and oppression of the nobility. The happy ending to this affair, in which the tragedy is averted through the Queen's intervention, concludes with a moralizing epilogue in which Greville stresses the larger theme of the episode: by Sidney's words and deeds in the quarrel and its aftermath, "he left an authentical president to after ages, that howsoever tyrants allow of no scope, stamp, or standard, but their own will; yet with Princes there is a latitude for subjects to reserve nature, & legall freedom, by paying huble tribute in manner, though not in matter, to them" (p. 81).

While the pith and point of the carefully shaped tennis court affair illustrate one facet of Greville's artistry, such compression alternates with the looser syntax and unhurried flow of the reflective passages which help create the impression that the *Life* is a rambling, discursive, and disorganized work. In fact, as discussed previously, it has a firm structure, but Greville's frequent asides and apologies, as in his request that "the Reader pardon me, if I presume yet againe to multiply digression upon Digression" (p. 185), suggest a looser, more digressive work than he actually wrote. Thus, Greville's ruminative tone, cumulative syntax, and nostalgic focus in the reflective portions of the work—*e.g.,* "Besides, I do ingenuously confess, that it delights me to keep company with him, even after death; esteeming his actions, words, and conversation, the daintiest treasure my mind could then lay up; or can at this day impart to our posteritie" (p. 138)—these combine to impart a superficial impression of rambling formlessness which tends to obscure the underlying firm and traditional structure of the *Life.*

In sum, Fulke Greville's *Life of Sr Philip Sidney* is an important work worthy of the modern reader's attention for a number of reasons. It is an invaluable source of original material about its subject, Philip Sidney, written by one who was in an unique position to know Sidney's thoughts and attitudes as well as his actions. The *Life* is also important, and indeed the most popular, work in the oeuvre of Greville, who has been "rediscovered" in the past quarter-century by critics as a major Renaissance author. And, finally, it is a major contribution to the emerging genre of English life-writing; Greville's *Life* illustrates the successful fusion of personal reminiscence and didactic purpose with traditional rhetorical structure. The result is a popular and important work which the present edition brings back into print in the form in which it first appeared.

WARREN W. WOODEN

Marshall University

# TEXTUAL NOTE

Several other editions of the *Life of Sidney* should be noticed as they relate to the present reproduction of the 1652 edition. In 1870, A. B. Grosart printed an edition using the Cambridge manuscript as his copy-text. Because of a faulty collation of the Cambridge version with the 1652 one and Grosart's failure to notice

many variants, this edition is not reliable. Nowell Smith's edition
of 1907 used the 1652 printed edition as his copy-text, collating
it with the Cambridge manuscript version and printing readings
from the latter when he felt them superior. Joaquin Kuhn's un-
published dissertation of 1973 is the first edition that attempts to
take into account the Shrewsbury manuscript version of the *Life*.
Kuhn selects his readings among the three versions of the *Life*,
using the Cambridge manuscript as his copy-text, but he was refused access to the other contemporary manuscript version of the
*Life*, that in the possession of Dr. B. E. Juel-Jensen of Oxford. In
sum, as of 1983 there is neither a reliable and comprehensive
scholarly edition of the *Life of Sidney* nor an accurate version of
the original 1652 edition in print. The present edition seeks to fill
at least one of these lacunae.

I am grateful to the William Oxley Thomas Memorial Library of
the Ohio State University for permission to reproduce their copy
of *The Life of the Renowned Sr Philip Sidney* (Wing B4899).

## NOTES

1. Greville's penchant for revising his works, together with his de-
cision not to commit them to print,
makes difficult both the dating and
establishment of final texts for his
works. I follow the general chronology of Greville's writings set forth
in G. A. Wilkes, "The Sequence of
the Writings of Fulke Greville,"
*Studies in Philology 56* (1959):
489-503, including his dating of the
*Life of Sidney* versions as 1609-14.

2. The standard biography of
Greville is Ronald A. Rebholz, *The
Life of Fulke Greville*, First Lord
Brooke (Oxford: Clarendon Press,
1971); it should be supplemented,
and occasionally corrected, by Joan
Rees, *Fulke Greville, Lord Brooke,
1554-1628: A Critical Biography*
(Berkeley: University of California
Press, 1971).

3. Rees, p. 58.

4. See page 2 of the present edition. All subsequent citations from
the *Life of Sidney* will be to this
edition with page references in-
cluded in the text.

5. Rees, pp. 62-63.

6. "He kept his manuscripts by
his side and engaged in what may
well have been perpetual revision.
Thus no chronology can be more
than approximate." F. J. Levy, "Fulke
Greville: The Courtier as Philo-
sophical Poet," *Modern Language
Quarterly 33*, no. 4 (December
1972), 435.

7. Brooke, Fulke Greville, Baron,
*Sir Fulke Greville's Life of Sir Philip
Sidney*, ed. Nowell Smith (Oxford:
Clarendon Press, 1907), p. xvii.

8. "A New Manuscript of Greville's 'Life of Sidney,'" *Modern
Language Review 49* (1954), 424-
27.

9. Joaquin C. Kuhn has a useful analysis and line-by-line breakdown of the material found in the Cambridge manuscript text and the printed text of 1652 but not in the Shrewsbury manuscript version of the *Life* in "An Edition of Fulke Greville's *Life of Philip Sidney*," Ph.D. diss., Yale University, 1973, pp. lxxix-lxxxviii.

10. In addition to the two previously discussed—Trinity College, Cambridge, R. 7, 32 and 32: *A Dedication to Sr. Philip Sidney and Shrewsbury Public Library*, Blakeway MS. 295 (untitled)—there is a third seventeenth-century manuscript of the *Life of Sidney*. This manuscript is the property of Dr. B. E. Juel-Jensen of Oxford. According to Mark L. Caldwell, in 1977 the manuscript was "currently being investigated by Mr. John Gouws of Lincoln College, Oxford." ("Sources and Analogues of the *Life of Sidney*," *Studies in Philology 74*[1977], 281). As of 1983, however, no description of the Oxford manuscript has appeared or been announced.

11. Thus, Joan Rees says "that it [the 1652/Cambridge ms. version] is later seems to be established by the fact that the printed text of the *Life* includes the story of Greville's thwarting over his projected history, whereas the Shrewsbury manuscript does not have this" (p. 76). Ronald Rebholz agrees that "It is nearly certain that the version represented by *S* [the Shrewsbury ms.] is the earlier of the two extant versions of the *Life*" (p. 333).

12. See especially Larson's discussion of theme in the *Life* at pp.

96-108 of his *Fulke Greville* (Boston: G. K. Hall, 1980).

13. See, for example, David A. Roberts's comments: "The figure of Sidney, man and poet, in the *Life* is consistently that of a paragon vanished from an imperfect world, one to which men can look to find both the ideal of poetry and the ideal in life. . . Sidney becomes a type of the presence of Divine Purpose in the world, in an age which seems, from the perspective of the *Life*, to be hopelessly remote." ("Fulke Greville's Aesthetic Reconsidered," *Studies in Philology 74* [1977], 390.)

14. Rees, p. 61.

15. Rebholz, p. 27. Rebholz's chapter, "Ideals of a Radical Protestant," pp. 17-31, provides a good overview of the Protestant program.

16. Indeed, Rebholz attributes the first publication of the *Life* to its censure of James's regime: "His attack on James's government by the standards of Elizabeth made the *Life of Sidney* tolerable to the Puritan England of 1652" (p. 323).

17. Stauffer, *English Biography Before 1700* (Cambridge: Harvard University Press, 1930), p. 141; Croll, *The Works of Fulke Greville* (Philadelphia: J.B. Lippincott, 1903), p. 52; Smith, p.v.

18. Kendall, *The Art of Biography* (New York: W. W. Norton, 1965), p. 93; Larson, p. 98.

19. Although some modifications have been suggested of the scheme he discerned as the basis for the *Apology*, most scholars assent to the argument put forth in 1935 by K. O. Myrick in *Sir Philip Sidney as a*

*Literary Craftsman* that the *Apology for Poetry* is modeled upon the demonstrative oration.

20. Thomas Wilson, *Wilson's Arte of Rhetorique,* 1560, ed. G. H. Mair (Oxford: Clarendon Press, 1909),

p. 4. (A reprint of the 1553 edition was published by Scholars' Facsimiles & Reprints in 1962 and reissued in 1977.)

21. *Ibid,* p. 13.

# THE LIFE
# Of the Renowned
## Sr *PHILIP SIDNEY.*

### WITH

The true Intereſt of *England*
as it then ſtood in relation to all Forrain Princes : And particularly for ſuppreſſing the power of *Spain* Stated by Him.

His principall Actions, Counſels,
Deſignes, and Death.

Together with a ſhort Account of
the Maximes and Policies uſed by Queen
*Elizabeth* in her Government.

Written by Sir F U L K E  G R E V I L
Knight, Lord Brook, a Servant to Queen
*Elizabeth,* and his Companion
& Friend.

*LONDON,*
Printed for *Henry Seile* over againſt St
*Dunſtans* Church in Fleet-ſtreet.
MDCLII.

Moſt humbly,
To the Right Honorable
THE
COUNTESSE
OF
SVNDERLAND.

Since Madam,

**B**Oth your Bloud, and Vertues do ſo ſtrong-ly Intitle you to this well-limb'd Piece; it would be a ſtain upon the Publiſher, to enſhrine it to any other *Name* but yours. *Who can protect the ſtory of a* Sidney, *but a* Sidney's *Name? Thus his* Matchleſs Poem, *ſeem'd providentially by him impatronag'd unto his* Peerleſs Siſter. *And this (Madam) being another of his* meaner Monuments, *diſdains Addreſs to any other Alliance but his own. Here at your feet (by no deſpicable Pen) the Hiſtory of our* Nations *Wonder lies ; Whoſe large ſpread Fame*

# Dedicatory.

Fame, your noble Meene im-
proves, and convinces the
World of this Truth, That
not only the Endowments of
Nature, but even the Enoble-
ments of the Mind, and Genius, are many times inherent
in the Bloud and Linage.
Some Families are privileg'd
from Heaven in Excellen-
cies, which now and then in
particular Branches, like new
Stars, appear and beautifie the
sphere they shine in And
doubtless if the departed into
Hap-

*Happiness*, *have any know-*
*ledge of our* humane Viciſsi-
tudes, *his gallant Soul looks*
*down with Contentment*, *to*
*ſee the* Honour *of his Houſe*
*continued in your* unblemiſht
Merit. *Which*, *taking all*,
*may excuſe the preſumption*
*that I can be charged with*,
*who not pretending to the Au-*
*thorage*, *have thought I could*
*not doe more right*, *either to*
*him*, *or the* ſubject *of the diſ-*
*courſe*, *than to inſcribe it to*
Her, *who like* day *in this* Ec-
clipſe

clipſe *of* Honour, *enlightning our* Weſtern Orb, *hath
ambition'd me to make this
offering from,*

Madam,

The meaneſt of your

moſt obedient Servants,

*P. B.*

The

# THE
# Life of the Renowned
## Sr *PHILIP SIDNEY*.

## *CHAP. I.*

THe difference which I have found between times, and confequently the changes of life into which their naturall viciffitudes doe violently carry men, as they have made deep furrowes of impreffions into my heart, fo the fame heavy wheeles caufe me to retire my thoughts from free traffique with the world, and rather feek comfortable eafe or imployment in the fafe memory of

B                    dead

dead men, than difquiet in a doubtfull converfation amongft the living.
Which I ingenuoufly confeffe, to be
one chief motive of dedicating
thefe exercifes of my youth to that
Worthy Sir *Philip Sidney*, fo long
fince departed. For had I grounded
my ends upon active Wifedomes of
the prefent, or fought Patronage out
of hope, or fear in the future ; Who
knowes not, that there are fome Noble friends of mine, and many Honourable Magiftrates yet livin g, un-
ro whom both my Fortune, and Reputation were, and are far more fubject ? But befides this felf-refpect of
Dedication, the debt I acknowledge
to that Gentleman is farre greater, as
with whom I fhall ever account it
honour to have been brought up :
and in whom the life it felf of true
worth, did ( by way of example ) far
exceed the pictures of it in any moral
Precepts. So that ( if my creation had
been equal ) it would have proved as
                                    eafie

f the world with any manner of
fparagement, the mifchance of
cknefle having caft fuch a kind of
eile over her excellent beauty, as
ne modefty of that fex doth many
mes upon their native, and heroi-
ll fpirits.

So that it may probably be gathe-
erd, that this clearneffe of his Fa-
ers judgement, and ingenious fen-
leneffe of his Mothers, brought
rth fo happy a temper in this well-
xt Ofspring of theirs, as (with-
t envy be it fpoken) Sir *Philip* de-
ves to be accompted amongft
ofe eminent Plants of our foyl,
ich blaft, or bite not, but rather
tuminate, and refrefh the Vines,
rn, Fruits, or whatfoever groweth
ler their fhaddows. And as he
their Firft-born, fo was he not
contraction, but the extenfion
heir ftrength, and the very aim,
perfect type of it.

Of whofe Youth I will report no
other

eafie for me, to have followed his
patern, in the practice of reall
vertue, as to engage my felf into
this *Characteriftical* kind of Poefie:
in defence whereof he hath written
fo much, as I fhall not need to fay a-
ny thing. For that this reprefenting
of vertues, vices, humours, counfells, and actions of men unfeigned,
and unfcandalous Images, is an in-
abling of free born fpirits to the
greateft affaires of States : he himfelf
hath left fuch an inftance in the too
fhort fcene of his life, as I fear many Ages will not draw a line out of
any other mans fphere to parallel
with it.

For my own part, I obferved, honoured, and loved him fo much ; as
with what caution foever I have paffed through my dayes hitherto a-
among the living, yet in him I challenge a kind of freedome even a-
mong the dead. So that although
with *Socrates*, I profeffe to know no-

B 2                    thing

thing for the prefent ; yet with *Ne-stor* I am delighted in repeating old newes of the ages paſt ; and will therefore ſtir up my drooping memory touching this mans worth, powers, waye, and deſignes : to the end that in the tribute I owe him, our nation may ſee a Sea-mark, rais'd upon their native coaſt, above the level of any private Pharos abroad : and ſo by a right Meridian line of their own, learn to ſayl through the ſtraits of true vertue, into a calm, and ſpacious Ocean of humane honour.

It is ordinary among men to obſerve the races of horſes, and breeds of other cattle. But few conſider, that as divers humors mixt in mens bodies make different complexions ; ſo every Family hath, as it were, divers predominant qualities in it : which, as they are tempered together in Marriage, give a certain tinĉture to all the deſcent. In my time, I have
observed

observed it in man
ly in this. Sir *Henry*
was a man of excel
large heart, ſweet
ſuch a Governour
make an end of the
but to plant his ov
ſperity of his Cou
found eſtabliſhme
and *Ireland*, whe
worthily grateful
unequall, & bitter
of Provincialls is
cere Monarchall
cially ſuch, as th
place ſuperior,
degrees of herald

On the other
ſhe was a woman
Nobility, ſo was
large ingenuous
were even ra
ſtrengths, ſhee
her ſelf from the
licate time, than

other wonder, but this ; That
though I lived with him, and knew
him from a child, yet I never knew
him other than a man : with fuch
ftaiedneffe of mind, lovely, and familiar gravity, as carried grace, and
reverence above greater years. His
talk ever of knowledge, and his very
play tending to enrich his mind : So
as even his teachers found fomething in him to obferve, and learn,
above that which they had ufually
read, or taught. Which eminence,
by nature, and induftry, made his
worthy Father ftile Sir *Philip* in my
hearing (though I unfeen) *Lumen fa-
miliæ fuæ.* But why doe I mention
this relative harmony of worth between Father and Son ? Did not his
Country foon after take knowledge
of him as a Light, or leading Star to
every degree within her ? Are not
the Arts and Languages, which enabled him to Travail at fourteen
years old, and in his Travail to win
reve-

reverence amongſt the chief Learned
men abroad, Witneſſes beyond exception, that there was great inequality of worth and goodneſſe in him?

Inſtance that reverend *Languet*,
mentioned for honours ſake in Sir
*Philip's Arcadia*, learned *uſque ad mi-
raculum*; wiſe by the conjunction of
practice in the world, with that well-
grounded Theory of Books, & much
valued at home; till this great
Worth ( even in a Gentleman fortune) being diſcovered for a dangerous inſtrument againſt *Rome* and
*Spain*, by ſome ſparkles got light e-
nough, rather to ſeek employment
elſwhere, than to tarry, and be driven out of his own Country with
diſparagement. In *Franckford* he
ſettles, is entertained Agent for the
Duke of *Saxony*, and an under-Land
Miniſter for his own King. Lodged he
was in *Wechels* houſe, the Printer of
*Franckford*, where Sir *Philip* in travail chancing likewiſe to become a
guest,

eafie for me, to have followed his
patern, in the practice of reall
vertue, as to engage my felf into
this *Characteriſticall* kind of Poefie:
in defence whereof he hath written
fo much, as I fhall not need to fay a-
ny thing. For that this reprefenting
of vertues, vices, humours, counfells, and actions of men unfeigned,
and unfcandalous Images, is an in-
abling of free born fpirits to the
greateft affaires of States : he himfelf
hath left fuch an inftance in the too
fhort fcene of his life, as I fear many Ages will not draw a line out of
any other mans fphere to parallel
with it.

For my own part, I obferved, honoured, and loved him fo much ; as
with what caution foever I have paffed through my dayes hitherto a-
among the living, yet in him I challenge a kind of freedome even a-
mong the dead. So that although
with *Socrates*, I profeffe to know nothing

thing for the prefent ; yet with *Ne-stor* I am delighted in repeating old newes of the ages paft ; and will therefore ftir up my drooping memory touching this mans worth, powers, waye , and defignes : to the end that in the tribute I owe him, our nation may fee a Sea-mark,rais'd upon their native coaft,above the le-vell of any private Pharos abroad : and fo by a right Meridian line of their own, learn to fayl through the ftraits of true vertue, into a calm, and fpacious Ocean of humane honour.

It is ordinary among men to obferve the races of horfes, and breeds of other cattle.But few confider,that as divers humors mixt in mens bodies make different complexions ; fo every Family hath, as it were, divers predominant qualities in it : which, as they are tempered together in Marriage , give a certain tincture to all the defcent. In my time, I have

obferved

of the world with any manner of difparagement, the mifchance of ficknefle having caft fuch a kind of veile over her excellent beauty, as the modefty of that fex doth many times upon their native, and heroicall fpirits.

So that it may probably be gathethered, that this clearnefle of his Fathers judgement, and ingenious fenfiblenefle of his Mothers, brought forth fo happy a temper in this wellmixt Ofspring of theirs, as (without envy be it fpoken) Sir *Philip* deferves to be accompted amongft thofe eminent Plants of our foyl, which blaft, or bite not, but rather ftatuminate, and refrefh the Vines, Corn, Fruits, or whatfoever groweth under their fhaddows. And as he was their Firft-born, fo was he not the contraction, but the extenfion of their ftrength, and the very aim, and perfect type of it.

Of whofe Youth I will report no
other

obferved it in many houfes, efpecially in this. Sir *Henry Sidney* his Father was a man of excellent naturall wit, large heart, fweet converfation : and fuch a Governour, as fought not to make an end of the State in himfelf, but to plant his own ends in the profperity of his Countrey. Witnes his found eftablifhments both in *Wales*, and *Ireland*, where his Memory is worthily gratefull unto this day: how unequall, & bitter foever the cenfure of Provincialls is ufually, againft fincere Monarchall Governours, efpecially fuch, as though in worth and place fuperior, are yet in their own degrees of heraldry, inferior to them.

On the other fide, his Mother, as fhe was a woman by defcent of great Nobility, fo was fhe by nature of a large ingenuous fpirit. Whence, as it were even racked with native ftrengths, fhee chofe rather to hide her felf from the curious eyes of a delicate time, than come up on the ftage

of

gueft, this ingenious old mans ful-
neſſe of knowledge, travailing as
much to be delivered from abundance by teaching, as Sir *Philip*'s rich
nature, and induſtry thirſted to be
taught, and manured; this harmony
of an humble Hearer to an excellent Teacher, ſo equally fitted
them both, as out of a naturall deſcent both in love, and plenty, the
elder grew taken with a net of his
own thread, and the younger taught
to lift up himſelf by a thread of the
ſame ſpinning; ſo as this reverend
*Languet*, orderly ſequeſtred from his
ſeverall Functions under a mighty
King , and *Saxonie* the greateſt
Prince of *Germany*, became a Nurſe
of knowledge to this hopefull young
Gentleman, and without any other
hire , or motive than this ſympathy
of affections, accompanyed him in
the whole courſe of his three years
travail. By which example the judicious Reader may ſee, that Worth

in

in every Nation finds her Country,
Parents, Neighbours, and Friends,
yea, and often, with more honour,
dearneffe, and advancement in
knowledges, than any pedigree of
fleſhly kindred, will, or can at home
raiſe, or enlarge them unto. Nay
to goe yet farther in this private inſtance ; It may pleaſe the Reader
to obſerve, how the ſame parallel
of worth, in what age, or eſtate
ſoever, as it hath power to win, ſo
hath it likewiſe abſolute power to
keep. Far unlike thoſe creations of
chance, which hath other birds
egges ; and by advancing men out of
chance or complement, loſe them
again as faſt by neglect. Contrary
to which, even when diverſity of
years, ccurſes of life, and fortunes,
enforced theſe dear Friends to di-
vide, there yet paſſed ſuch a continuall courſe of intelligence by Letters from one of them to another, as
in their loſſe (if they be loſt) there be
buried

buried many delicate images , and
differences, between the reall, and
large complexions of thofe active
times, and the narrow *falves* of this
effeminate age : Becaufe in this excellent mould of their friendfhip, the
greateft bufinefles of Eftate were fo
mixed with the fweet remiffions of
ingenuous good will, as men might
eafily difcern in them ( as unflatte-
ring glaffes ) that wifdome, and love,
in good fpirits have great affinity together. For a farther demonftration,
behold even the fame *Languet* ( after
he was fixty fix years of age ) fafhio-
ning himfelf a journey into *England*,
with the Duke *Cafimire*, onely to fee
that excellent Plant of his own poli-
fhing. In which loving, aud unexpected meeting , I dare confidently
affirm, neither fide became lofer. At
the fea they parted, and made many
mutuall tears omnious propheciers
of their never meeting again.

Thefe little fparks of two large
natures

natures I make bold the longer to infift upon, becaufe the youth, life and fortune of this Gentleman were indeed but fparkes of extraordinary greatneffe in him: which for want of clear vent lay concealed, and in a maner fmothered up. And again to bring the children of favor, and change, into an equall ballance of comparifon with birth, worth, and education and therein abruptly to conclude, that God creates thofe in his certain, and eternall mouldes, out of which he elects for himfelf, where Kings choofe creatures out of *Pandoras* Tun, and fo raife up worth, and no worth; friends or enemies at adventure. Therefore what marvail can it be, if thefe *Iacobs*, and *Efaus* ftrive ambitioufly one with another, as well before as after they come out of fuch erring, and unperfect woulbes?

Now from chefe particular teftimonies to goe on with Sir *Philips* life

life: though he purpofed no monuments of books to the world, out of
this great harveft of knowledge; yet
doe not his Arcadian Romanties live
after him, admired by our foure-
eyd Criticks? who, howfoever their
common end upon common arts be
to affect reputation by depraving
cenfure; yet where nature placeth
excellencie above envy, there (it
feemeth) fhe fubjecteth thefe carping eyes to wander, and fhewes the
judicious reader, how he may be
nourifhed in the delicacy of his own
judgement.

For inftance; may not the moft
refined fpirits, in the fcope of thefe
dead images(even as they are now)
finde, that when Soveraign Princes, to play with their own vifions,
will put off publique action, which
is the fplendor of Majeftie, and unactively charge the managing of
their greateft affaires upon the fe-
cond-hand faith, and diligence of
                              Deputies,

Deputies, may they not ( I say ) understand, that even then they bury themselves, and their Estates in a cloud of contempt, and under it both encourage and shaddow the the conspiracies of ambitious subalternes to their false endes, I mean the ruine of States and Princes?

Again, where Kingly Parents will suffer, or rather force their wives and daughters, to descend from the inequality and reservednesse of Princely education, into the contemptible familiarity, and popular freedome of Shepherds; may we not discern that even therein they give those Royall birthes warrant, or opportunity, to break over all circles of honor, safe-guards to the modesty of that sex; and withall make them fraily, apt to change the commanding manners of Princely Birth, into the degrading images of servile basenesse? Lastly, where humor takes away this pomp, and

*appa-*

*apparatus* from King, Crown, and
Scepter, to make fear a Counfellor,
and obfcurity a wifdom ; be that
King at home what the current , or
credit of his former Goverment, for a
a while, may keep him: yet he is fure
among forrain Princes to be juftly
cenfured as a Princely Shepherd , or
Shepherdifh King : which creatures
of fcorn feldome fail to become fit
facrifices for home-born difcontent-
ments , or ambitious forrain fpirits
to undertake, and offer up.

Againe, who fees not the chance-
able arrivall of *Euarchus* into *Arcadia* ; his unexpected election to the
temporary Soveraignty of that State;
his fitting in a cloudy feat of judgement, to give fentence ( under a
mafk of Shepherds ) againft his Son,
Nephew, Neeces, the immediate fucceffors to that Scepter; and all accu-
fed and condemned of rape , pari-
cide, adulteries, or treafons, by their
own Lawes: I fay who fees not, that
thefe

thefe dark webs of effeminate Princes be dangerous forerunners of innovation, even in a quiet, and equally tempered people? So that if Sir *Philips* had not made the integrity of this forrain King an image of more conftant, pure, and higher ftrain, than nature makes thofe ordinary mouldes, wherein fhe fafhioneth earthly Princes, even this opportunity, and map of defolation prepared for *Euarchus*, wherein he faw all the fucceffors of this Province juftly condemned under his own fentence, would have raifed up fpecious rights, or pretences for new ambition in him; and upon the never-failing pillars of occafion amafednes of people, and fad offer of glorious novelties, have tempted him to eftablifh this Election for a time, fucceffively, to him and his for ever?

To be fhort, the like, and finer moralities offer themfelves throughout
                                        that

that various, and dainty work of his,
for founder judgements to exercife
their Spirits in; fo that if the infancie
of thefe *Ideas* , determining in the
firft generation, yield the ingenuous
Reader fuch pleafant & profitable di-
verfity, both of flowers, and fruits, let
him conceive, if this excellent Image-
maker had liv'd to finifh , and bring
to perfection this extraordinary
frame of his own Common-wealth:
I meane, the return of *Bafilius* , from
his dreames of humor, to the honor
of his former Eftate; the marriage of
the two fifters with the two excellent Princes ; their iffue; the warres
ftirred up by *Amphialus*; his marriage
with *Helena* ; their fucceffions; together with the incident Magnificen-
ces, pompes of ftate, providences of
councells in treaties of peace, or aliance, fummons of warres , and orderly execution of their diforders ; I
fay , what a large field an active able
fpirit fhould have had to walk in, let
C the

the advifed Reader conceive with grief. Efpecially if he pleafe to take knowledge, that in all thefe creatures of his making, his intent, and fcope was, to turn the barren Philofphy precepts into pregnant Images of life; and in them, firft on the Monarch's part, lively to reprefent the growth, ftate, and declination of Princes, change of Government, and lawes: viciffitudes of fedition, faction, fucceffion, confederacies, plantations, with all other errors, or alterations in publique affaires. Then again in the fubjects cafe; the ftate of favor, diffavor, profperitie, adverfity, emulation, quarrell, undertaking, retiring, hofpitality, travail, and all other moodes of private fortunes, or misfortunes. In which traverfes ( I know ) his purpofe was to limn out fuch exact pictures, of every pofture in the minde, that any man being forced, in the ftraines of this life, to pafs through any ftraights, or

lati-

latitudes of good, or ill fortune,
might (as in a glasse) see how to let
a good countenance upon all the dif-
countenances of adverfitie, and a
ftay upon the exorbitant fmiling of
chance.

Now, as I know this was the firft
project of thefe workes, rich (like
his youth)in the freedome of affections, wit, learning, ftile, form, and
facilitie, to pleafe others: fo muft I
again (as ingenuoufly) confefs,
that when his body declined, and his
piercing inward powers were lifted
up to a purer Horizon, he then difcovered, not onely the imperfecti-
on, but vanitie of thefe fhadowes,
how daintily foever limned: as feeing that even beauty it felf, in all
earthly complexions, was more apt
to allure men to evill, than to fafhion
any goodnefs in them. And from
this ground, in that memorable teftament of his, he bequeathed no o-
ther legacie, but the fire, to this un-

C 2                     polifhed

polifhed Embrio. From which fate
it is onely referved, untill the world
hath purged away all her more grofs
corruptions.

Again, they that knew him well,
will truly confefs, this *Arcadia* of his
to be, both in form, and matter, as
much inferior to that unbounded
fpirit of his, as the induftry and Images of other mens works, are many
times raifed above the writers capacities : and befides acknowledge, that
howfoever he could not choofe but
give them many afperfions of fpirit,
and learning from the Father ; yet
that they were fcribled: rather as
pamphlets, for entertainment of
time, and friends, than any accompt of himfelf to the world. Becaufe if his pupofe had been to
leave his memory in books, I am
confident, in the right ufe of Logick,
Philofophy, Hiftory, and Poëfie, nay
even in the moft ingenuous of Mechanicall Arts, he would have fhew
ed

ed fuch tracts of a fearching, and judicious fpirit; as the profeſſors of
every faculty would have ſtriven no
lefs for him, than the feaven Cities
did to have *Homer* of their Sept! But
the truth is : his end was not writing, even while he wrote; nor his
knowledge moulded for tables, or
ſchooles; but both his wit, and un-
derſtanding bent upon his heart , to
make himſelf, and others, not in
words or opinion, but in life , and
action, good and great.

In which Architectonical art he was
fuch a Maſter, with fo commending,
and yet equall waies amongſt men,
that wherſoever he went, he was beloved, and obeyed : yea into what
Action foever he came laſt at the
firſt, he became firſt at the laſt ; the
whole managing of the bufinefs, not
by ufurpation, or violence, but ( as
it were ) by right, and acknowledg-
ment, falling into his hands, as into
a naturall Center.

G 3        By

By which onely commendable
monopolie of alluring, and improving men, how the same drawes all
windes after it in fair weather : so
did the influence of this spirit draw
mens affections and undertakings to
depend upon him.

✦✦✦✦✦✦✦✦✦✦✦✦✦✦✦✦✦✦✦✦✦✦

## CHAP. II.

HEre I am still enforced to bring
pregnant evidence from the
dead: amongst whom I have found
far more liberall contribution to the
honor of true worth , than among
those which now live ; and in the
market of selfnesse, traffique new
interest by the discredit of old
friends: that ancient wisdome of
righting enemies, being utterly worn
out of date in our modern discipline.

My first instance must come from
that

that worthy Prince of *Orange*, *Willi-am* of *Naſſau*, with whom this young Gentleman having long kept intelligence by word, and letters, and in affaires of the higeſt nature that then paſſed currant upon the ſtages of *England*, *France*, *Germany*, *Italy*, the low Countries, or *Spaine*, it ſeemes that this young Gentleman had, by his mutuall freedome, ſo imprinted the extraordinary merit of his young yeares into the large wiſdome, and experience of that excellent Prince, as I paſſing out of *Germany* into *England*, and having the unexpected honor to finde this Prince in the Town *Delph*, cannot think it unwelcome to deſcribe the clothes of this Prince; his poſture of body, and minde, familiarity, and reſervedneſs to ths ingenuous Reader, that he may ſee with what diverſe Characters Princes pleaſe, and Govern Cities, Townes, and Peoples.

His uppermoſt garment was a
C 4                    gown,

gown, yet such as ( I dare confidently affirm ) a mean-born student, in
our Innes of Court, would not have
been well-pleafed to walk the ftreets
in. Unbuttoned his doubled was,
and of like precious matter, and
form to the other. His waft-coat
(which fhewed it felf under it) not
unlike the beft fort of thofe wollen
knit ones, which our ordinary wa-
termen row us in  His Company a-
bout him, the Burgeffes of that beer-
brewing Town : and he fo fellow-
like encompaffed with them, as
( had I not known his face ) no ex-
terior figne of degree. or deferved-
nefs could have difcovered the inequality of his worth or Eftate from
that multitude  Notwithftanding I
no fooner came to his prefence, but
it pleafed him to take knowledge of
me. And even upon that ( as if it had
been a fignall to make a change) his
refpect. of a ftranger inftantly begat
refpect to himfelf in all about him:

An

An outward paſſage of inward
greatneſs, which in a popular E-
ſtate I thought worth the obſerving.
Becauſe there, no pedigree but
worth could poſſibly make a man
Prince, and no Prince, in a moment,
at his own pleaſure.

The buſineſſes which he then
vouchſafed to impart with me were,
the dangerous fate which the Crown
of *England*, States of *Germany*, and
the Low Countries did ſtand threatned with, under an ambitious
and conquering Monarch's hand.
The main inſtance, a ſhort deſcrip-
on of the Spaniards curious affecting
to keep the Romans waies, and
ends, in all his actions. On the other
ſide, the clear ſymptomes of the
Hectique feaver, univerſally then
reigning among the Princes of
Chriſtendome, ordain'd ( as he
thought ) to behold this undermining diſeaſe without fear, till it
ſhould prove dangerous, nay incu-
rable

rable to them. This active King of
*Spain* having put on a mask of conscience, to cover an invisible conjunction between the temporal, and spi-
ritual ambitions, of these two sometimes creeping, sometimes commanding Romish and Spanish Conquerors. The particulars were many,
both excellent and enlightning.

As first, the fatall neutrality of
*France*, jealous of the Spanish greatness, as already both wrong'd, and
threatned by it : and yet their Kings
so full of pleasures, and consequently
so easily satisfied with the complements of words, treaties, or alliances,
and since the fall of the *Sorbonists*,
their own exempted Church so ab-
solutely possest, and govern'd by the
Jesuits ; as through the bewithing liberties, and bondages of Auricular
confession, they were rather wrought
to rest upon a vain security of reputed strength, than really to hazzard
loss, and help themselves by diversion, or assailing.                    Again,

Againe, on the Queens part, by the
way of queſtion, he ſuppoſed a little
neglect in her Princely mildneſs,
while ſhe did ſuffer a Proteſtant party, rais'd by God in that great Kingdome of *France*, to be a ballance or
counterpeaſe to that dangerous *Hep-*
*tarchy of Spain* ( then ſcarce viſible,
but ſince multiplyed by an unreſiſt-
able greatneſſe ) I ſay, for ſuffering
this ſtrong and faithfull party
(through want of imployment) to
ſink into it ſelf, and ſo unactively
(like a Meteor) to vaniſh, or ſmother
out, in vain and idle apparitions.
Withall reverently hee demurr'd,
whether it were an omiſſion in that
excellent Ladies Government, or no,
by a remiſſe looking on, whilſt the
*Auſtrian* aſpiring family framed occaſion to gain by begging peace, or
buying war from the Grand Signior;
and both exceeding much to their
own ends; In reſpect that once in
few years, this Emperor made himſelf

felf Generall by it, over all the forces of Chriftendome; and thereby
gained the fame of action; trained
up his owne Inftruments Martially,
and got credit with his fellow-bor-
dering Princes, through the common Councell, or participation of
fear. Befides that in the conclufions
of peace, he ever faved a mafs of
riches gather'd by Diets, Contributi-
ons, Devotions, and Levies for common defence, which out of the ill-ac-
compting hand of war, became (in
his Exchequer) Treafure, to terrifie
even thofe Chriftian neighbours that
did contribute to it. And the more
efpecially he infifted upon this: becaufe all thofe crafty Pageants of her
enemies were difguifedly acted, even
whilft her Majefty had an Agent of
extraordinary diligence, worth, and
credit with that vaft Eftate of Tur-
kie, into whofe abfolute and imperious fpirit, without any further
charge than infufing the jealoufies of
com-

competition, thefe practifes among
thofe Auftrian ufurpers, might eafily
have been interrupted.

Laftly, it pleafed him to queftion
yet a greater over-fight in both thefe
Kingdoms, *England*, and *France* : Becaufe while their Princes ftood at
gaze, as upon things far off, they ftill
gave way for the Popifh, and Spanifh
invifible Arts, and Counfels, to un-
dermine the greatnefs, and freedom
both of Secular and Ecclefiafticall
Princes : a mortall ficknefs in that
vaft body of *Germany*, and by their
infenfible fall, a raifing up of the
houfe of *Auftria* many fteps towards
her long affected Monarchy over the
Weft. The ground of which opinion
was (as he thought) in refpect that
even the Catholique Princes, and Bi-
fhops themfelves ( had their eyes bin
well wakened) would never have en-
dured any cloud, or colour of Religion, to hape changed their Princely
Soveraignties into fuch a kind of
low,

low, and Chaplaine tenure : as fince
they have fleepily fallen into : but
would rather have ftirred them with
many hands, to binde this Miter-fu-
perftition, with the reall cords of
truth. And to that end perchance
have fet *Spain* on work with her
new, and ill digefted Conquefts: her
dangerous enemie *Fefs* : her native
*Moors*, and *Iews* ( fince craftily
tranfported ) and fo probably have
troubled the ufurpations both of the
*Pope*, and *Spain*, over that well-tem-
pered, though over-zealous, and fuperftitions Region of *Italy*. Thefe,
and fuch other particulars, as I had
in charge, and did faithfully deliver
from him to her Majefty, are fince
performed, or perifhed with time, or
occafion.

The laft branch was his free ex-
preffing of himfelfe in the honour of
Sir *Philip Sidney*, after this manner :
That I would firft commend his
own humble fervice, with thofe
fore-

fore-mentioned Ideas to the Queen ;
and after crave leave of her freely to
open his knowledge, and opinion of
a Fellow-fervant of his, that (as he
heard) lived unimployed under her.
With himfelfe he began *ab ovo*, as having been of *Charles* the fift's Privie
Counfell, before he was one and
twenty years of age : and fince ( as
the world knew) either an Actor, or
at leaft acquainted with the greateft
actions, aud affairs of *Europe* ; and
likewife with her greateft men, and
minifters of Eftate. In all which fe-
ries of time, multitude of things,
and perfons, he protefted unto mee
( and for her fervice) that if he could
judge, her Majefty had one of the ri-
peft, and greateft Counfellors of E-
ftate in Sir *Philip Sidney*, that at this
day lived in *Europe* : to the triall of
which hee was pleafed to leave his
owne credit engaged, untill her Majefty might pleafe to employ this
Gentleman , either amongft her
friends or enemies.  At

At my return into *England*, I performed all his other comandments ; this that concerned Sir *Philip* (thinking to make the fine-fpun threads of Friendfhip more firm between them) I acquainted Sir *Philip* with : not as queftioning, but fully refolved to doe it. Unto which he at the firft fight oppofing, difcharged my faith impawn'd to the Prince of *Orange*, for the delivery of it ; as an act only entending his good, and fo to be perform'd, or difpens'd with at his pleafure ; yet for my fatisfaction freely added thefe words:firft, that the Qu. had the life it felf daily attending her : and if fhe either did not, or would not value it fo highly, the commendation of that worthy Prince could be no more(at the beft) than a lively picture of that life, and fo of far leffe credit, and eftimation with her. His next reafon was, becaufe Princes love not that forrain Powers fhould have extraordinary

in their Subjects ; much lesse to be
taught by them how they should
place their own: as arguments either
upbraiding ignorance, or lack of
large rewarding goodnefs in them.
This Narration I adventure of, to
shew the clearnefs, and readinefs of
this Gentlemans judgement, in all
degrees,and offices of life : with this
farther teftimony of him ; that after
mature deliberation being once refolved, he never brought any queftion of change to afflict himfelf with,
or perplex the bufinefs ; but left the
fuccefs to his will, that governs the
blinde profperities, and unprofperi-
ties of Chance ; and fo works out his
own ends by the erring frailties of
humane reafon and affection. Laftly,
to manifeft that thefe were not complements, felf-ends, or ufe of each o-
ther,according to our modern fafhion but meer ingenuities of fpirit, to
which the ancient greatnefs of hearts
ever frankly engaged their Fortunes,
D                      let

let Actions, the lawfully begotten children, equall in spirit, shape, and complexion to their parents,be testimonies ever sufficient.

My second instance comes from the Earle of *Leicester* his unckle,who told me ( after Sir *Philips*, and not long before his own death ) that when he undertook the government of the Low Countries, he carryed his Nephew over with him , as one amongst the rest, not only despising his youth for a Counsellor, but withall bearing a hand over him as a forward young man. Notwithstanding, in short time he saw this Sun so risen above his Horizon, that both he and all his Stars were glad to fetch light from him. And in the end acknowleged that he held up the honor of his casual authority by him,whilst he lived,& found reaso to withdraw himself from that burthen,after his death.

My third record is Sir *Francis Walsingham* his Father-in-law ; that wife,

Treasons against us, acknowledged openly; That howsoever he was glad King *Philip* his Master had lost, in a private Gentleman, a dangerous Enemy to his Estate; yet he could not but lament to see Christendome depriv'd of so rare a Light in these cloudy times; and bewail poor Widdow *England* (so he term'd her) that having been many years in breeding one eminent spirit, was in a moment bereaved of him, by the hands of a villain.

Indeed he was a true modell of Worth; A man fit for Conquest, Plantation, Reformation, or what Action soever is greatest, and hardest amongst men. Withall, such a lover of Mankind, and Goodnesse, that whosoever had any reall parts, in him found comfort, participation, and protection to the uttermost of his power; like *Zephyrus* he giving life where he blew. The Universities abroad, and at home, accompted him

wise, and active Secretarie. This man ( as the world knows ) upheld both Religion and State, by using a policy wisely mixt with reflexions of either. He had influence in all Countries, & a hand upon all affairs, Yet even this man hath often confessed to my self, that his *Philip* did so far overshoot him in his own Bow, as those friends which at first were Sir *Philip*'s for this Secretaries sake, within a while became so fully owned, and possest by Sir *Philip*, as now he held them at the second hand, by his Son-in-laws native courtesie.

This is that true remission of mind, whereof I would gladly have the world take notice from these dead mens ashes: to the end that we might once again see that ingenuity amongst men, which by liberall bearing witnesse to the merits of others, shews they have some true worth of their own; and are not meerly lovers of themselves, without rivals.

D 2                    *CHAP.*

❧❧❧❧❧❧❧❧❧❧❧❧❧❧❧❧❧❧❧❧❧❧

## CHAP. III.

TO continue this paſſage a little
further: I muſt lift him above
the cenſure of Subjects, and give
you an account what reſpect ,
and honour his worth wanne him a-
mongſt the moſt eminent Monarchs
of that time As firſt with that chief,
and beſt of Princes, his moſt excellent Majeſty, then King of *Scotland*,
to whom his ſervice was affectio-
nately devoted, and from whom he
received many pledges of love, and
favour.

In like manner, with the late renowned *Henry* of *France*, then of *Navarre*, who having meaſured , and
maſtered all the ſpirits in his own
Nation, found out this Maſter-ſpirit
among us, and uſed him like an e-
quall in nature, and ſo fit for friend-
ſhip with a King.                    A-

Again, that gallant Princ
*John de Auſtria*, Vice-Roy
Low Countries for *Spain*, wh
Gentleman in his Embaſſage
Emperor came to kiſs his
though at the firſt, in hi
haughture, he gave him acc
deſcent to a youth, of grac
ſtranger, and in particular
tion (as he conceived) to a
yet after a while that he
his juſt altitude, he fou
ſo ſtricken with this ext
Planet, that the beholder
to ſee what ingenuous
brave, and high minded
to his worth ; giving
and reſpect to this ho
Gentleman , than to
dors of mighty Prince
But to climb yet a
In what due eſtimati
dinary Worth was,
nemies, will appea
When *Mendoza*, a S
                    D

him a generall *Mecænas* of Learning;
Dedicated their Books to him; and
communicated every Invention, or
Improvement of Knowledge with
him. Souldiers honoured him, and
were so honoured by him, as no man
thought he marched under the true
Banner of *Mars*, that had not obtai-
ned Sir *Philip Sidney's* approbation.
Men of Affairs in most parts of Christendome, entertained correspon-
dency with him. But what speak I
of these, with whom his own waies,
and ends did concur? since ( to descend ) his heart, and capacity were
so large, that there was not a cun-
ning Painter, a skilfull Engenier, an
excellent Musician, or any other Ar-
tificer of extraordinary fame that
made not himself known to this famous Spirit, and found him his true
friend without hire; and the common *Rende-vous* of Worth in his
time.

   Now let Princes vouchsafe to consider,

sider, of what importance it is to the
honour of themselves, and their E-
states, to have one man of such eminence; not onely as a nourisher of
vertue in their Courts, or service;but
besides for a reformed Standard, by
which even the most humorous persons could not but have a reverend
ambition to be tried, and approved
currant.   This I doe the more confidently affirm, becaufe it will be
confessed by all men, that this one
mans example, and personall respect,
did not onely encourage Learning,
and Honour in the Schooles, but
brought the affection, and true use
thereof both into the Court, and
Camp. Nay more, even many Gentlemen excellently learned amongst
us will not deny, but that they affected to row, and steer their course
in his wake. Besides which honour
of unequall nature, and education,
his very waies in the world, did
generally adde reputation to his
                              Prince,

Prince, and Country, by reftoring
amongft us the ancient Majeftie of
noble, and true dealing: As a manly
wifdome, that can no more be
weighed down, by any effeminate
craft, than *Hercules* could be over-
come by that contemptible Army of
Dwarfs. This was it which, I pro-
fefs, I loved dearly in him, and ftill
fhall be glad to honour in the great
men of this time: I mean, that his
heart and tongue went both one
way, and fo with every one that
went with the Truth; as knowing
no other kindred, partie, or end.

Above all, he made the Religion
he profeffed, the firm Bafis of his life:
For this was his judgement (as he
often told me) that our true-heart-
edneffe to the Reformed Religion
in the beginning, brought Peace,
Safetie, and Freedome to us; concluding, that the wifeft, and beft
way, was that of the famous *William*
Prince of *Orange*, who never divided
the

the confideration of Eftate from the
caufe of Religion, nor gave that
found party occafion to be jealous,
or diftracted, upon any apparance of
fafety whatfoever; prudently refolving, that to temporize with the E-
nemies of our Faith, was but (as a-
mong Sea-guls) a ftrife, not to keep
upright, but aloft upon the top of
every billow: Which falfe-hearted-
neffe ro God and man, would in the
end find it felf forfaken of both;
as Sir *Philip* conceived. For to this
active fpirit of his, all depths of the
Devill proved but fhallow fords;
he piercing into mens counfels, and
ends, not by their words, oathes, or
complements, all barren in that
age, but by fathoming their hearts,
and powers, by their deeds, and
found no wifdome where he found
no courage, nor courage without
wifdome, nor either without hone-
fty and truth. With which folid,
and active reaches of his, I am perfwaded,

swaded, he would have found, or made a way through all the traverses, even of the moſt weak and irregular times. But it pleaſed God in this decrepit age of the world, not to reſtore the image of her ancient vigour in him, otherwiſe than as in a lightning before death.

Neither am I ( for my part ) ſo much in love with this life, nor believe ſo little in a better to come, as to complain of God for taking him, and ſuch like exorbitant worthyneſs from us : fit (as it were by an Oſtraciſme) to be divided, and not incorporated with our corruptions : yet for the ſincere affection I bear to my Prince, and Country, my prayer to God is, that this Worth, and Way may not fatally be buried with him ; in reſpect, that both before his time, and ſince, experience hath publiſhed the uſuall diſcipline of greatnes to have been tender of it ſelf onely ; making honour a triumph, or rather
trophy

trophy of defire, fet up in the eyes
of Mankind, either to be worfhiped
as Idols, or elfe as Rebels to perifh
under her glorious oppreffions,
Notwithftanding, when the pride of
flefh, and power of fa vour fhall ceafe
in thefe by death, or difgrace; what
then hath time to regifter, or fame to
publifh in thefe great mens names,
that will not be offenfive, or infecti-
ous to others ? What Peril without
blotting can write the ftory of their
deeds? Or what Herald blaze their
Arms without a blemifh ? : And as
for their counfels and projects when
they come once to light, fhalb they
not live as noyfome, and loath fome-
ly above ground, as their Authors
carkaffes lie in the grave? So as the
return of fuch greatnes to the world,
and themfelves, can be but private
reproach, publique ill example, and
a fatall fcorn to the Government
they live in. Sir *Philip Sidney* is none
of this number; for the greatnefs
　　　　　　　　　　　　which

which he affected was built upon
true Worth; esteeming Fame more
than Riches, and Noble actions far
above Nobility it self.

✤✿✤✿✤✿✤✿✤✿✤✿✤✿✤✿✤✿✤✿✤✿✤✿✤✿✤✿

## CHAP. IV.

ANd although he never was Magiftrate, nor poffeffed of any fit
ftage for eminence to act upon, wher-
by there is fmall latitude left for
comparing him with thofe deceafed
Worthies, that to this day live un-
envied in ftory; Yet can I probably
fay, that if any fupreme Magiftra-
cie; or employment, might have
fhewed forth this Gentlemans
Worth, the World fhould have
found him neither a mixt *Lyfander*,
with unactive goodnefs to have corrupted indifferent Citizens; nor yet
like that gallant Libertine *Sylla*, with

a

a tyrannizing hand, and ill example, to have ordered the diffolute
people of *Rome*; much lefs with that
unexperienced *Themiftocles*, to have
refufed, in the feat of Juftice, to
deale equally between friends and
ftrangers. So that as we fay, the
abftract name of goodnefs is great,
and generally currant; her nature
hard to imitate, and diverfly wor-
fhipped, according to Zones, complexions, or education; admired by
her enemies, yet ill followed by her
friends: So I may well fay, that this
Gentlemans large, yet uniform dif-
pofition was every where praifed;
greater in himfelf than in the world;
yet greater there in fame and honour
than many of his fuperiors; reverenced by forrain Nations in one form,
of his own in another; eafily cenfured, hardly imitated; and therefore
no received Standard at home, becaufe his induftry, judgement, and
affections, perchance feemed too

great

great for the cautious wifdomes of
little Monarchies to be fafe in. Notwithftanding, whofoever will be
pleafed indifferently to weigh his
life, actions, intentions, and death,
fhall find he had fo fweetly yoaked
fame and confcience together in a
large heart, as inequality of worth,
or place in him, could not have been
other than humble obedience, even
to a petty Tyrant of *Sicily*. Befides,
this ingenuitie of his nature did
fpread it felf fo freely abroad, as who
lives that can fay he ever did him
harm ; whereas there be many living, that may thankfully acknowledge he did them good ? Neither
was this in him a private, but a publique affection ; his chief ends being
not Friends, Wife, Children, or himfelf ; but above all things the honour
of his Maker, and fervice of his
Prince, or Country.

　Now though his fhort life, and
private fortune, were (as I fayd) no
proper

proper ftages to act any greatnefs of good, or evill upon; yet are there ( even from thefe little centers of his ) lines to be drawn, not Aftrono-micall, or imaginary, but reall linea-ments, but fuch as infancy is of mans-eftate; out of which nature often fparkleth brighter rayes in fome, than ordinarily appear in the ripe-nefs of many others. For proof wher-of, I will pafs from the teftimonie of brave mens words, to his own deeds. What lights of founder wif-dome can we afcribe to our greateft men of affairs than he fhewed in his youth, and firft employment, when he was fent by the late *Queen* of fa-mous memory, to condole the death of *Maximilian*, and congratulate the fucceffion of *Rodolph* to the Empire? For under the fhaddow of this com-plement between Princes, which forted better with his youth than his fpirit, Did he not, to improve that journey, and make it a reall fervice

to

to the Empire? For under the fhadow of this complement between
Princes, which forted better with
his youth than his fpirit, did he not,
to improve that journey, and make
it a real fervice to his Soveraigr, pro-
cure an Article to be added to his
Inftructions, which gave him fcope
(as he paíled) to falute fuch *German*
Princes, as were interefted in the
caufe of our Religion, or their own
native liberty?

And though to negotiate with that
long-breathed Nation proves commonly a work in fteel, where many
ftroaks hardly leave any print; yet
did this Mafter *Genius* quickly ftir
up their cautious, and flow judgements to be fenfible of the danger
which threatned them hourely, by
this fatall conjunction of *Rome*'s undermining fuperftitions, with the
commanding forces of *Spain*. And
when he had once awaked that confident Nation to look up, he as ea-

sily made manifest unto them, that
neither their inland seat, vast multitude, confused strength, wealth, nor
hollow-founding Faine could secure
their Dominions from the ambition
of this brave aspiring Empire; howsoever by the like helps they had
formerly bounded the same Roman,
and Austrian supremacies. The reasons he alleged were, because the
manner of their conjunction was not
like the ancient undertakers, who
made open war by Proclamation;
but craftily (from the infusion of
*Rome*) to enter first by invisible traffique of souls; filling peoples minds
with apparitions of holines, specious
Rites, Saints, Miracles, institutions of
new Orders, reformations of old,
blessings of Catholiques, cursings of
Heretiques, Thunder bolts of Excommunication under the authority
of their Mother Church. And when
by these shadows they had gotten
possession of the weak, discouraged
                                    the

the strong, divided the doubtful, and finely lulled inferior powers asleep; as the ancient Romans were wont to tame forrain nations with the name *Socij*, then to follow on with the Spanish, less spirituall, but more forcible Engines, *viz.* practice, confederacy, faction, money, treaties, leagues of traffique, alliance by marriages charge of rebellion, war, and all other acts of advantagious power.

Lastly he recalled to their memories, how by this brotherhood in evill (like *Simeon*, and *Levi*) *Rome* and *Spain* had spilt so much bloud, as they were justly become the terror of all Governments; and could now be withstood, or ballanced by no other means, than a general league in Religion: Constantly and truely affirming, that to associate by an uniform bond of conscience, for the protection (as I said) of Religion, and Liberty, would prove a more solid union, and symbolize far better a-

E 2                      gainst

gainſt their Tyrannie , than any Factious combination in policy, league
of ſtate, or other traffique of Civill,
or Martial humors poſſibly could do.

To this end did that undertaking
ſpirit lay, or at leaſt revive the foundation of a league between us, and
the *Germ..n* Princes, which continues
firme to this day : The defenſive part
whereof hath hitherto helped to
ſuport the ruines of our Church a-
broad, and diverted her enemies
from the ancient ways of hoſtility,
unto their *Conclave*, and modern undermining Arts. So, that if the offenſive part thereof had been as well
proſecuted in that true path, which
this young *Genius* trod out to us ;
both the paſſage for other Princes o-
ver the *Alps*, would have been by this
time more eaſie than *Hanibal's* was ;
and beſides , the firſt ſound of that
Drum might happily have reconciled thoſe petty dividing Schiſmes
which reign amongſt us ; not as
　　　　　　　　　　　ſprung

sprung from any difference of religious Faith, but misty Opinion; and
accordingly moulded first upon the
Desks of busie idle Lecturers, then
blown abroad to our disadvantage
by a swarm of Popish Instruments,
rather Jesuits than Christians; and to
their ends most dangerously over-
spreading the world, for want of a
confident Moderator. This (I say)
was the first prize which did enfran-
chise this Master Spirit into the my-
steries, and affairs of State.

❀❀❀❀❀ ❀❀❀❀❀ ❀❀❀❀❀ ❀❀❀❀❀❀

## *CHAP. V.*

THe next doubtfull Stage hee
had to act upon ( howsoever it
may seem private) was grounded upon a publique and specious propo-
sition of marriage, between the late
famous Queen, and the Duke of *An-*
*iou*, With which Current, although
he saw the great, and wise men of the

E 3                    time

time fuddainly carryed down, and
every one fifhing to catch theQueens
humor in it; yet when he confidered
the difference of years perfon, education, ftate, and religion between
them; and then called to minde the
fuccefs of our former alliances with
the *French*; he found many reafons
to make queftion whether it would
prove Poetical, or reall on their part?
And if reall; yet whether the ballance
fwayed not unequally, by adding
much to them, and little to his Soveraign? The Dukes greatnefs being onely name, and poffibility; and
both thefe either to wither, or be
maintained at her coft. Her ftate a-
gain in hand; and though Royally
fufficient to fatisfie that Queens
Princely and moderate defires, or ex-
pences, yet perchance inferior to bear
out thofe mixt defignes, into which
his ambition, or neceffities might entife, or draw her.

Befides, the marriage of K. *Philip*,
to

to Q. *Mary* her fifter, was yet fo frefh in memory, with the many inconveniences of it, as by comparing and paralleling thefe together, he found credible inftances to conclude, neither of thefe forrain alliances could prove fafe for this Kingdom. Becaufe in her marriage with *Spain*, though both Princes continuing under the obedience of the *Roman* Church, neither their confciences, nor their peoples could fuffer any fear of tumult; or imputation by change of faith; Yet was the winning of St. *Quintins*, with the lofs of *Calice*, and the carrying away of our money to forrain ends, odious univerfally; the *Spanifh* pride incompatible; their advantagious delayes fufpicious; and their fhort reign here felt to be a kinde of exhaufting tax upon the whole Nation.

Befides, he difcerned how this great Monarch countenanced with our Forces by fea, and land, might, and
E 4      did

did ufe this addition of her ftrength
to transform his Low-Countrey
Dukedomes, fall'n to him by defcent, into the nature of a foveraign
conqueft;and fo by conjoyning their
Dominion, and Forces by Sea, to his
large Empires,and Armies upon the
Mayn, would probably enforce all
abfolute Princes to acknowledg fubjection to him before their time. And
for our Kingdome, befides that this
King then meant to ufe it as a forge,
to fafhion all his foveraign defignes
in;had he not(except fome bely him)
a fore-running hand in the change of
Religion after King *Edwards* death ?
And had he not(even in that change)
fo maftered us in our own Church,
by his Chaplain and Conclave of
*Rome,*that both thefe carried all their
courfes byaced to his ends, as to an
elder brother, who had more abundant degrees of wealth, and honour
to return them ? fo as every body
(that devoted Queen excepted)fore-
                                    faw

faw we muft fuddenly have been compelled to wear his livery, and ferve his ends; or elfe to live like children neglected, or disfavoured by our holy Mother.

Again, for our temporall Government; was not his influence (except report belie him) as well in paffing many fharp lawes, and heavy executions of them with more ftrange Councels; as fashioning our leagues both of peace, and traffique to his conquering ends? All thefe together, with that Mafter prize of his playing, when under colour of piety, he ftirred up in that wel-affected Queen a purpofe of reftoring thofe temporalities to the Church, which by the fall of Abbies, were long before difperfed among the Nobility, Gentry, and people of this Kingdome: all thefe (as he faid) did clearly fhew, that this ambitious King had an intent of moulding us to his ufe, even by diftracting us amongft our felves.

Never-

Neverthelesse, to give him the honor of worldly wisedom, I dare aver; he had no hope of bringing these curious assumptions to pass; but rather did cast them out, as sounding lines, to fathome the depths of peoples mindes; and with particular fear, and distraction in the owners, to raise a generall distast in all men against the Government. Now, if we may judge the future by what is past, his scope in all these particulars could be no other, but when our inward waters had been throughly troubled, then to possess this diversly diseas'd Estate with certain poëticall titles of his own , devised long before, and since published by *Dolman*, to the end, that under the shadow of such clouds, he might work upon the next heir; and so cast a chance for all our goodes, lives, and liberties with little interruption. These, and such like, were the groundes which moved Sir *Philip* to

com-

compare the paſt, and preſent con-
ſequence of our Marriage with either of theſe Crowns together.

And though in danger of ſubjecti-
on he did confeſs our aliance with
the French to be leſſe unequall ;
yet even in that, he foreſaw, diver-
ſitie of Religion would firſt give
ſcandall to both ; and in progreſs,
prove fatall of neceſſity to one ſide.
Becauſe the weaker ſect here, being
fortified by ſtrong parties abroad,
and a husbands name at home, muſt
neceſſarily have brought the native
Soveraign under a kinde of Covert
Baron   and thereby forced her Majeſty, either to loſe the freedom, and
conſcience of a good Chriſtian, the
honor of an excellent Prince, or the
private reputation of obedient Wife.
Neither could that excellent Lady
( as he, and that time conceived )
with theſe, or any other cautions,
have countermined the mines of
practice, whereby ( it is probable )

this

this Prince would have endeavoured to steal change of Religion into her Kingdom.

1. As first, by cavelling at the Authors, and Fathers that upheld her Church.

2. Then by disgracing her most zealous Ministers, through aspersions cast upon their persons, and advancing indifferent spirits, whose God is this world, the Court their heaven, and consequently their ends, to biace Gods immortall truth to the fantasies of mortall Princes.

By the subtile latitude of school-distinctions, publiquely edging nearer the holy mother Church; and therein first waving, then sounding the peoples mindes; if not with abrupt, and spirit-fall'n tolleration, yet with that invisible web of connivencie, which is a snare to entangle great, or little flies, at the will of power.

4. By a Princely licentiousnesse in beha-

behaviour, and conference, fashioning atheisme among her Subjects :
as knowing that in confusion of
thoughts, he might the more easilie
raise up superstitious idolatry :
which crafty Image of his, with all
the nice lineaments belonging to it,
was the more credible, in respect the
French have scornfully affirm'd one
chief branch of our Princes prerogatives to be, the carying of their
peoples consciences which way they
list. An absolutenes the more dangerous to their subjects freedom, because they bring these changes to
pass ( as the French say ) under the
safe conduct of our earth-cy com.
mon law; and thereby make change
legally safe, and constancie in the
truth exceeding dangerous.

　5. By a publique decrying of our
ancient Customes, and Statutes; and
from that ground, giving Proclamations a Royall vigor in moulding of
pleas, pulpits and Parliaments after
　　　　　　　　　　　　the

the pattern of their own, and some other forain Nations; which in our Government is a confusion, almost as fatall as the confusion of tongues.

6. By employing no instruments among the people, but such as devise to sheer them with taxes, ransome them with fines, draw in bondage uuder colour of obedience, and ( like Frenchified *Empsons*, and *Dudlies* ) bring the English people to the povertie of the French Peasants, onely to fill up a *Danaus* sive of prodigality, and thereby to secure the old age of Tyranny from that which is never old: I mean, danger of popular inundations.

To lift up Monarchie above her ancient legall Circles, by banishing all free spirits, and faithfull Patriots, with a kinde of shaddowed Ostracisme, till the *Ideas* of native freedom should be utterly forgotten; and then ( by the pattern of their own Duke of *Guise* ) so to encourage

courage a multitude of impoverifhing impofitions upon the people, as he might become the head
of all difcontentednefs; and under
the envy of that art, ftir them up to
depofe their naturall annointed Soveraign,

8. When he had thus metamor-
phofed our moderate form of Monarchie into a precipitate abfolute-
nefs; and therein fhaken all Leagues
offenfive or defenfive between us,
the Kings of *Denmark,* and *Sweden*,
the free Princes of *Garmany,* the
poor oppreffed foules of *France*, the
fteady fubfifting *Hanfes*; and laftly
weakned that league of Religion,
fuffique, which with profperous fuccefs hath continued long between
us, and the *Netherlanders*; then ( I
fay ) muft his next project have
been, either abufively to entife, or
through fear enforce this excellent
Lady, to countenance his over-
grown party abroad by fuffering the
fame

same sect to multiply here at home, till she should too late discover a necessity, either of changing her faith, hazarding her Crown, or at least holding it at the joint courtesie of that ambitious Roman Conclave, or encreasing Monarchie of *Spain.* A Scepter, and Miter, whose conjunction bringes forth boundless freedom to themselves, and begets a narrow servitude upon all other Nations, that by surprise of wit, or power become subject to them.

9 Besides, in the practice of this Marriage, he foresaw, and prophesied, that the very first breach of Gods ordinance, in matching herself with a Prince of a diverse faith, would infallibly carry with it some piece of the rending destiny, which *Solomon*, and those other Princes justly felt, for having ventured to weigh the immortall wisdom in even scales, with mortall conveniency or inconveniency.

10. The

10. The next ſtep muſt infallibly have been ( as he conceived ) with our ſhipping to diſturb or beleaguer the *Netherlanders* by Sea, under colour, or pretence of honor unſeaſonably taken, even when the horſe and foot of *France* ſhould threaten their ſubſiſtence by land ; and therby ( in this period of extremity ) conſtrain that active people to run headlong into one of theſe three deſperate courſes, *viz.* Either to fly for protection to the Flower-de-Luce, with whom they join in continent; Or precipitately ſubmit their necks to the yoking Cittadells of *Spain*, againſt whoſe inquiſitions, and uſurpations upon their Conſciences, and Liberties, ſo much money, and bloud had been ſhed, and conſumed already; Or elſe unnaturally to turn Pirates, and ſo become enemies to that trade, by which they and their friends have reciprocally gotten, and given ſo much proſperity.

F                 The

The choice or comparifon of which mifchiefes to them, and us, he briefly laid before me , in this manner.

Firft , that if they fhould incorporate with *France*, the *Netherlands* manufactures, induftry, trade , and fhipping , would add much to that Monarchie, both in peace, and war: The naturall riches of the French having been hitherto either kept barrain at home , or barrainly tranfported abroad , for lack of the true ufe of trade , fhipping, exchange, and fuch other myfteries as multiply native wealth ; by improving their man-hood at home , and giving formes both to domeftique , and forrain materialls; which defect ( as he faid ) being now abundantly to be fupplied , by this conjunction with the *Netherlands*, would in a little time , not onely puff up that active Common-wealth with unquiet pride , but awake the ftirring

French

French to feel this addition to their
own ftrengths ; and fo make them
become dangerous neighbours by
incurfion in invafion to the Baltique
Sea ; many waies prejudice to the
mutuall trafflque between *Italy*, the
*Germans* , and *England* ; and confequently a terror to all others , that
by land, or Sea confine upon them,
yea and apt euough once in a year,
to try their fortune with that growing Monarch of *Spain*, for his Indian
treafure.

2. On the other fide; if any ftricter
league fhould come to pafs between
thofe adventurous French Spirits ,
and the folid counfells of *Spaine* ;
and fo through fear , fcorn , or
any other defperate apparances
force the *Netherlands* into a precipitate , but fteady fubjection of that
Spanifh Monarchie ; then he willed
me to obferve, how this fearfull union of Earth, and Sea, having efca-
ped the petty Monarches of *Europe*,

would

would in all probability, coſtrain them to play after-games for their own Eſtates. Becauſe theſe two potent Navies ( his and the *Netherland's* ) being thus added to his invincible Armies by land , would ſoon ( as he thought ) compell that head of holy mother Church, whoſe beſt uſe for many yeares had been (by ballancing theſe two Emperiall greatneſſes one with another ) to ſecure inferior Princes : would ( as I ſaid ) ſoon enforce that ſacred Mother-head to ſhelter her ſelf under the wings of this Emperiall Eagle , and ſo abſolutely quit her Miter-ſupremacie ; or at leaſt become Chaplain to this ſuppreſſing, or ſupporting Conqueror.

Beſides , in this fatall probability he diſcovered the great difference between the wiſdom of quiet Princes, in their moderate deſires of ſubſiſtence, from the large , and hazardous counſells of undertaking Mo-

Monarches; whofe ends are onely to make force the umpier of right, and by that inequality become Soveraign Lords ( without any other title ) over equalls and inferiors.

3. Now for this third point , of conftraining this oppreffed , yet active *Netherland* people to become Pirates: he willed me in the examples of time paft to obferve , how much *Scirpalus* did among the Grecians ; *Sextus Pompeius* the Romans , even in their greatnefs ; and in the modern, *Flufhiug, Dunkerk , Rochell* and *Algiers*. Inferring withall, th at this people , which had fo long profpered upon the rich materialls of all Nations, by the two large fpreading armes of manufacture , and traffique , could not poffibly be forced at once to leave this habit : but would rather defperately adventure to maintain thefe enriching ftrengthes of marriners, fouldiers, and fhipping of their own, with

be-

becomming a Rende-vous for the
fwarm of difcontented fubjects univerfally ; inviting them with hope
of fpoil, and by that inheritance, to
try whether the world were ready
to examine her old foundations of
freedom, in the fpecious, and flattering regions of change, and Powers
encrochments ?

Laftly, befides this uneven ballance
of State ; the very reflexion of fcorn
between age, and youth ; her come-
linefs, his difadvantage that way ;
the exceffive charge by continuall
refort of the French hither ; danger
of change for the worfe ; her reall
native States and riches made fubject to forrain humors ; little hope
of fucceffion, and if any, then
*France* affured to become the feat,
and *England* the Province ; children,
or no children, misfortune, or uncer-
tainty : Thefe ( I fay) and fuch like
threatning probabilities made him
joyn with the weaker party, and
oppofe

oppofe this torrent; even while the French faction reigning had caft afperfions upon his Uncle of *Leicefter*, and made him, like a wife man (under colour of taking phyfick) voluntarily become prifoner in his chamber.

✤✤✤✤✤✤✤✤✤✤✤✤✤✤✤✤✤✤✤✤✤✤✤

## CHAP. VI.

THus ftood the ftate of things then : And if any judicious Reader fhall afk, Whether it were not an error, and a dangerous one, for Sir *Philip* being neither Magiftrate nor Counfellor, to oppofe himfelf againft his Soveraigns pleafure in things indifferent? I muft anfwer, That his worth, truth, favour, and fincerity of heart, together with his reall manner of proceeding in it, were his privileges. Becaufe this Gentlemans courfe in this great bufi-

F 4                              nefs

nefs was, not by murmur among e-
quals, or inferiours, to detract from
Princes ; or by a mutinous kind of
bemoaning error, to ftir up ill affections in their minds , whofe beft
thoughts could do him no good ; but
by a due addrefs of his humble reafons to the *Queen* her felf, to whom
the appeal was proper.   So that although he found a fweet ftream of
Soveraign humors in that well-tem-
pered Lady, to run againft him, yet
found he fafety in her felf, againft
that felfnefs which appeared to
threaten him in her : For this happily born and bred Princefs was not
(fubject-like) apt to conftrue things
reverently done in the worft fenfe ;
but rather with the fpirit of annointed Greatnefs ( as created to reign
equally over frail and ftrong ) more
defirous to find waies to fafhion her
people, than colours, or caufes to punifh them.

Laftly, to prove nothing can be
wife,

wife, that is not really honeſt; every man of that time, and confequently of all times may know, that if he ſhould have uſed the ſame freedome among the Grandees of Court (their profeſſion being not commonly to diſpute Princes purpoſes for truths fake, but fecond their humours to govern their Kingdomes by them) he muſt infallibly have found Worth, Juſtice, and Duty lookt upon with no other eyes but *Lamia's*; and ſo have been ſtained by that reigning faction, which in all Courts allows no faith currant to a Soveraign, that hath not paſt the feal of their practiſing corporation.

Thus ſtood the Court at that time; and thus ſtood this ingenuous ſpirit in it. If dangerouſly in mens opinions who are curious of the preſent, and in it rather to doe craftily, than well : Yet, I fay, that Princely heart of hers was a Sanctuary unto him; And as for the people, in whom many

ny times the lasting images of Worth
are preferred before the temporary
visions of art, or favour, he could not
fear to suffer any thing there, which
would not prove a kind of Trophy
to him. So that howsoever he seemed to stand alone, yet he stood upright ; kept his access to her Majesty
as before ; a liberall conversation
with the *French*, reverenced amongst
the worthiest of them for himselfe,
and born in too strong a fortification
of nature for the less worthy to ab-
bord, either with question, familiarity, or scorn.

In this freedome, even while the
greatest spirits, and Estates seemed
hood-winkt, or blind ; and the inferior sort of men made captive by
hope, fear, ignorance ; did he enjoy
the freedome of his thoughts, with
all recreations worthy of them.

And in this freedome of heart being one day at Tennis, a Peer of this
Realm, born great, greater by alliance,

ance, and fuperlative in the Princes favour, abruptly came into the Tennis-Court ; and fpeaking out of thefe three paramount authorities, he forgot to entreat that, which he could not legally command. When by the encounter of a fteady object, finding unrefpectivenefs in himfelf (though a great Lord) not refpected by this Princely fpirit, he grew to expoftulate more roughly. The returns of which ftile comming ftill from an underftanding heart, that knew what was due to it felf, and what it ought to others, feemed (through the mifts of my Lords paffions, fwoln with the winde of his faction then reigning) to provoke in yeelding. Whereby, the leffe amazement, or confufion of thoughts he ftirred up in Sir *Philip,* the more fhadowes this great Lords own mind was poffeffed with : till at laft with rage (which is ever ill-difciplin'd) he commands them to depart the Court. To this

Sir

Sir *Philip* temperately anfwers ;
that if his Lordfhip had been pleafed
to exprefs defire in milder Chara-
&ters, perchance he might have led
out thofe, that he fhould now find
would not be driven out with any
fcourge of fury. This anfwer (like a
Bellows) blowing up the fparks of
excefs already kindled, made my
Lord fcornfully call Sir *Philip* by the
name of Puppy. In which progrefs
of heat, as the tempeft grew more and
more vehement within, fo did their
hearts breath out their perturbations
in a more loud and fhrill accent. The
*French* Commiffioners unfortunately
had that day audience, in thofe private Galleries, whofe windows look-
ed into the Tennis-Court. They inftantly drew all to this tumult: every fort of quarrels forting well with
their humors, efpecially this. Which
Sir *Philip* perceiving, and rifing with
inward ftrength, by the profpe&t of a
mighty fa&tion againft him; asked
my

my Lord, with a loud voice, that
which he heard clearly enough before. Who (like an Echo, that ftill
multiplies by reflexions) repeated
this Epithet of Puppy the fecond
time. Sir *Philip* refolving in one anfwer to conclude both the attentive
hearers, and paffionate actor, gave my
Lord a Lie, impoffible (as he aver-
red) to be retorted; in refpect all the
world knows, Puppies are gotten by
Dogs, and Children by men.

Hereupon thofe glorious inequalities of Fortune in his Lordfhip were
put to a kinde of paufe, by a precious inequality of nature in this
Gentleman. So that they both ftood
filent a while, like a dumb fhew in a
Tragedy; till Sir *Philip* fenfible of
his own wrong, the forrain, and factious fpirits that attended; and yet,
even in this queftion between him,
and his fuperior, tender to his Countries honour; with fome words of
fharp accent, led the way abruptly
out

out of the Tennis-Court; as if so un-expected an accident were not fit to be decided any farther in that place. Whereof the great Lord making a-nother fense, continues his play, without any advantage of reputati-on; as by the standard of humours in those times it was conceived.

A day Sr *Philip* remains in suspense, when hearing nothing of, or from the Lord, he sends a Gentleman of worth to awake him out of his trance; wherein the *French* would assuredly think any pause, if not death, yet a lethargy of true honour in both. This stirred a resolution in his Lordship to send Sir *Philip* a Challenge. Not-withstanding, these thoughts in the great Lord wandred so long between glory, anger, and inequality of state, as the Lords of her Majesties Coun-sell took notice of the differences, commanded peace, and laboured a reconciliation between them. But needlesly in one respect, and boot-
lesly

lefly in another. The great Lord being (as it fhould feem) either not ha-
fty to adventure many inequalities
againft one , or inwardly fatisfied
with the progrefs of his own Acts :
Sir *Philip* on the other fide confident,
he neither had nor would lofe, or
let fall any thing of his right. Which
her Majefties Counfell quickly perceiving, recommended this work to
her felf.

The Queen , who faw that by the
lofs, or difgrace of either , fhe could
gain nothing, prefently undertakes
Sir *Philip*; and (like an excellent Monarch)lays before him the difference
in degree between Earls,and Gentlemen ; the refpect inferiors ought to
their fuperiors ; and the neceffity in
Princes to maintain their own creations,as degrees defcending between
the peoples licentioufnefs,and the a-
noynted Soveraignty of Crowns :
how the Gentlemans neglect of the
Nobility taught the Peafant to in-
fult upon both.          Where-

Whereunto Sir *Philip* , with such
reverence as became him, replyed :
First, that place was never intended
for privilege to wrong : witness her
self, who how Soveraign soever she
were by Throne, Birth, Education,
and Nature; yet was she content to
cast her own affections into the same
moulds her Subjects did, and govern
all her rights by their Laws. Again,
he besought her Majesty to consider,
that although he were a great Lord
by birth, alliance, and grace; yet hee
was no Lord over him : and therfore
the difference of degrees between
free men, could not challenge any o-
ther homage than precedency. And
by her Fathers Act (to make a Princely wisdom become the more familiar) he did instance the Government
of K. *Henry* the eighth, who gave the
Gentry free, and safe appeal to his
feet, against the oppression of the
Grandees; and found it wisdome, by
the stronger corporation in number,

to

to keep down the greater in power : inferring elfe, that if they fhould u-nite, the over-grown might be tempted, by ftill coveting more, to fall (as the Angels did) by affecting equality with their Maker.

This conftant tenor of truth he took upon him; which as a chief duty in all creatures, both to themfelves, & the foveraignty above them, protected this Gentleman ( though he obeyed not) from the difpleafure of his Sove-raign. Wherein he left an authentical prefident to after ages, that howfoe-ver tyrants allow of no fcope, ftamp, or ftandard, but their own will ; yet w^th Princes there is a latitude for fub-jects to referve native, & legall free-dom, by paying humble tribute in manner, though not in matter, to them.

❧❧❧❧❧ ❧❧❧❧❧❧❧❧❧❧❧❧❧❧❧❧❧❧❧

## CHAP. VII.

THE next ftep which he intend-ded into the world, was an ex-
G pedition

pedition of his own projecting;
wherein he fashioned the whole body, with purpose to become head of
it himself. I mean the last employment but one of Sir *Francis Drake* to
the West Indies. Which journey, as
the scope of it was mixt both of sea,
and land service; so had it accordingly distinct Officers, & Commanders,
chosen by Sir *Philip* out of the ablest
Governors of those Martiall times.
The project was contrived between
themselves in this manner; that both
should equally be Governours, when
they had left the shore of *England*;
but while things were a preparing at
home, Sir *Fran.* was to bear the name,
and by the credit of Sir *Phil.* have all
particulars abundantly supplyed.

The reason of which secret carri-
age was, the impossibility for Sir
*Philip* to win the Queen, or Government (out of the value which they
rated his worth at) to dispense with
an employment for him so remote,
and

and of so hazardous a nature. Besides
his credit, and reputation with the
State lay not that way. So as our
provident Magistrates expecting a
Prentiship more seriously in Martial,
than Mechanical actions; and therein
measuring all men by one rule; would
(as Sir *Philip* thought) not easily believe his unexperience equall for a
designe of so many divers, and dangerous passages : howsoever wise
men , even in the most active times
have determined this art of Government, to be rather a riches of nature,
than any proper fruit of industry, or
education. This (as I said ) was one
reason, why Sir *Philip* did cover that
glorious enterprize with a cloud. Another was , because in the doing,
while it past unknown , he knew it
would pass without interruption ;
and when it was done , presumed the
success would put envy and all her
agents to silence.

On the other side Sir *Francis* found

that

that Sir *Philip*'s friends, with the influence of his excellent inward powers, would add both weight, and fashion to his ambition ; and consequently either with, or without Sir *Philip*'s company, yeeld unexpected eafe, and honor to him in this voiage.

Upon thefe two divers Counfels they treat confidently together ; the preparations go on with a large hand amongft our Governors ; nothing is denyed Sir *Francis* that both their propounding hearts could demand. To make which expedition of lefs difficulty, they kept the particular of this plot more fecret than it was poffible for them to keep the generall preparations of fo great a journey ; hoping that while the *Spaniard* fhould be forced to arm every where againft them, he could not any where be fo royally provided to defend himfelf, but they might land without any great impediment.

In thefe termes Sir *Francis* departs

from

from *Plimouth* with his ſhips; vowed
and reſolved that when he ſtaid for
nothing but for a wind, the watch
word ſhould come poſt for Sir *Philip.*
The time of the year made haſte a-
way, & Sr *Francis* to follow it, either
made more haſte than needed, or at
leaſt ſeemed to make more than really he did. Notwithſtanding, as I
dare aver that in his own element he
was induſtrous; ſo dare I not con-
demn his affections in this miſpriſion
of time. Howſoever a letter comes
poſt for Sir *Philip,* as if the whole
fleet ſtayed onely for him, and the
wind. In the mean-ſeaſon the State
hath intelligence that *Don Antonio*
was at ſea for *England,* and reſolved
to land at *Plimouth.* Sir *Philip* turning
occaſion into wiſdome, puts himſelf
into the imployment of conducting
up this King; and under that veil
leaves the Court without ſuſpicion;
over-ſhoots his father-in-law then
Secretary of Eſtate in his own bow;

G 3                    comes

comes to *Plimmouth*; was feasted the first night by Sir *Francis*, with a great deale of outward Pomp and complement.

Yet I that had the honor as of being bred with hm from his youth; so now ( by his own choice of all *England* ) to be his loving, and beloved *Achates* in this journey, observing the countenance of this gallant mariner more exactly than Sir *Philips* leisure served him to doe; after we were laid in bed , acquainted him with my observation of the discountenance, and depression which appeared in Sir *Francis*; as if our coming were both beyond his expectation, and desire. Neverthelesse that ingenuous spirit of Sir *Philip's*, though apt to give me credit, yet not apt to discredit others, made him suspend his own, & labor to change, or qualifie my judgement; Till within some few daies after , finding the shippes neither ready according to pro-

promife, nor poffibly to be made ready in many daies; and withall obferving fome fparcks of falfe fire, breaking out unawares from his yoke-fellow daily; It pleafed him (in the freedom of our friendfhip) to return me my own ftock, with intereft.

All this whlie *Don Antonio* landes not; the fleet feemed to us (like the weary paffengers Inn)ftill to goe further from our defires; letters came from the Court to haften it away: it may be the leaden feet, and nimble thoughts of Sir *Francis* wrought in the day, and unwrought by night; while he watched an opportunity to difcover us, without being difcovered.

For within a few daies after a poft ftealesup to the Court, upon whofe arrivall an Alarum is prefently taken: meffengers fent away to ftay us, or if we refufed, to ftay the whole Fleet. Notwithftanding this firft

*Mer-*

*Mercury*, this errand being partly advertifed to Sir *Philip* beforehand, was intercepted upon the way; his letters taken from him by two refolute fouldiers in Marriners apparell; brought inftantly to Sir *Philip*, opened, and read. The contents as welcome as Bulls of excommunication to the fuperftitious Romanift, when they enjoyn him either to forfake his right, or his holy Mother-Church, yet did he fit this firft proceffe, without noife, or anfwer.

The next was a more Imperiall Mandate, carefully conveyed, and delivered to himfelf by a Peer of this Realm; carrying with it in the one hand grace, the other thunder. The grace was an offer of an inftant imployment under his Unckle, then going Generall into the Low Countries; Againft which although he would gladly have demurred; yet the confluence of reafon, tranfcendencie of Power, fear of ftaying the
whole

whole Fleet, made him inftantly fa-
crifife all thefe falfe places to the duty of obedience.

Wherein how unwillingly foever
he yeelded up his knowledge, affections, publique and private endes in
that journey; yet did he act this
force in a gallant fafhion. Opens his
referved ends to the Generall; en-
courageth the whole Army with
promife of his uttermoft affiftance;
faves Sir *Francis Drake* from blaft-
ings of Court, to keep up his reputation amongft thofe companies which
he was prefently to command; clea-
reth the dafeled eyes of that Army,
by fhewing them, how even in that
forrain imployment, which took
himfelf from them, the Queen had
engaged herfelf more waies than one
againft the Spaniards ambition: fo
as there was no probability of taking
away her Princely hand from fuch a
well-ballanced work of her own.

Neverthelefe as the Limmes of
*Venus*

*Venus* picture, how perfectly soever
began, and left by *Apelles*, yet after
his death proved impossible to fi-
nish: so that *Heroicall* design of invading, and possessing *America*, how
exactly soever projected, and digest-
ed in every minute by Sir *Philip*, did
yet prove impossible to be well acted
by any other mans spirit than his
own; how sufficient soever his associate were in all parts of navigation;
whereby the success of this journey
fell out to be rather fortunate in
wealth, than honor.

Whereupon, when Sir *Philip* found
this, and many other of his large,
and sincere resolutions imprisoned
within the pleights of their fortunes,
that mixed good, and evill together
unequally; and withall discerned,
how the idle-censuring faction at
home had won ground of the active
adventures abroad; then did this
double depression both of things,
and men, lift up his active spirit into

to an univerfall profpect of time,
States, and things: and in them
made him confider, what impoffibi-
lity there was for him, that had no
delight to reft idle at home, of re-
propounding fome other forrain en-
terprife, probable, and fit to invite
that excellent Princeffes minde, and
moderate Government, to take hold
off. The placing of his thoughts upon
which high pinnacle, layd the prefent Map of the Chriftian world un-
derneath him.

## *CHAP. VIII.*

IN which view, nature guiding his
eyes, firft to his Native Country,
he found greatnefs of worth, and
place, counterpoyfed there by the
arts of power, and favor. The ftir-
ing fpirits fent abroad as fewell, to
keep the flame far off: and the ef-
femi-

feminate made judges of danger
which they fear, and honor which
they underſtand not.

The people (by diſpoſition of the
clime) valiant, and multiplying,
apt indifferently to corrupt with
peace, or refine with action; and
therefore to be kept from ruſt, or
mutiny, by no meanes better than by
forrain employments. His opinion
being that *Ilanders* have the air and
waters ſo diverſly moving about
them, as neither peace, nor war, can
long be welcome to their humors,
which muſt therefore be govern d by
the active, and yet ſteady hand of
authority. Beſides he obſerved the
Sea to have ſo naturall a Sympathie,
with the complexions of them ſhe
invirons, as be it in traffique, pira-
cie, or war, they are indifferent to
wander upon that element; and for
the moſt part apter to follow undertaking chance, than any ſetled endes
in a Marchant-traffique.

Now

Now for the blefled *Lady* which
then governed over us: how equall
foever fhe were in her happy creation for peace, or war, and her people
( as I have fhewed ) humble to follow her will in either, yet becaufe
fhe refolved to keep within the *De-*
*corum* of her fex, fhe fhewed herfelf
more ambitious of ballancing neighbor Princes from invading one another, than under any pretence of
title, or revenge, apt to queftion or
conquer upon forrain Princes pof-
feffions. And though this moderate
courfe carried her into a defenfive
war, which commonly falls out rather to be an impoverifhing of enemies, than any meanes to enrich,
or difcipline their Eftates that undertake it; yet could not all the
rackes of lofs, injury, or terror, ftir
this excellent *Lady* into any further
degree of offenfive war, than onely
the keeping of her Navy abroad, to
interrupt the fafe-comming home of
his

his *Indian* Fleet, and hinder the provision, contracted for in all parts of *Europe*, to furnish another invincible Navy, wherewith he purposed to besiege the world, and therein (as his first step) her divided Kingdomes.

On the other side, in this survay of forrain Nations, he observed a fatall passivenesse generally currant by reason of strange inequalities between little humors and great fortunes in the present *Princes* reigning.

Amongst whom for the first object *Henry* the third of *France* appeares to him in the likeness of a good Master, rather than a great King; buried in his pleasures, his Crown demain exhausted impositions multiplyed, the people light, the Nobility prone to move, and consequently his Country apt, through scorn of his effeminate Vices either to become a prey for the strongest undertaker, or else to be Cantonized by

self

self-divifion. In both which poffible
difafters, their native wealth, and
variety of objects, perchance have
made both King, and people ( howfoever confufedly erring ) yet to
live fecured by the providence of
chance.

Again, he faw the vaft body of the
Empire refting(as in a dream ) upon
an immoveable centre of felf-great-
nefs; and under this falfe affumpfit,
to have laid the bridle on the neck
of the Emperor, to work them arti-
ficially, with a gentle, or fteady hand,
to his own will.

And to confirm, and multiply
this clowdy danger, he difcerned
how that creeping Monarchie of
*Rome* ( hy her Arch-inftruments the
Iefuits ) had already planted fine
Schooles of ferving humanity in di-
verfe of their reformed Cities: intending fo to tempt this welbelieving
people, with that old forbidden tree
of knowledge, as they might fin defperately

perately againſt their own Eſtates,
before they knew it.

The like miſt theſe crafty-raiſers
invented ( as he thought ) to caſt o-
ver that well-united fabrick of the
*Hanſes*: whoſe endes being meerly
wealth, and their ſeats invironed on
every ſide with active, and power-
full neighbors, would ( in all probability ) make them as jealous of abſolute Princes in proſperity, as zealous in diſtreſs to ſeek protection
under them. So that they being at
this time grown mighty by combination, if they ſhould be neglected,
would prove apt, and able to ſway
the bailance unequally to the endes
of the ſtronger.

Beſides, he diſcerned yet a greater,
and more malignant aſpect from
that ſpreading Monarchie of *Spain*;
which abſolutely commanding the
houſe of *Auſtria*, governing the *Conclave*, and having gotten, or affecting to get a commanding intelli
gence

gence over thefe Cities; would foon
multiply unavoidable danger, both
to themfelves, and us, by mixing the
temporall, and fpirituall fword, to
their crafty conquering ends.

Nay more; how upon the fame
foundation they had begunne yet
a more dangerous party, even a-
mongft the German Princes themfelves; by adding to the fatall oppo-
fition of Religion between them,
the hopes, feares, jealoufie, temptations of reward, or lofs, with all the
unnaturall feeds of divifion; which
might make them, through thefe
confufed threatnings, and extice-
ments, to become an eafie prey for
the Spaniards watchfull, unfa-
tiable, and much promifing ambition.

He likewife obferved, *Battorie* that
gallant man, but dangeroufly afpiring King of *Poland*, to be happily
peifed by the ancient competition
between him, and his Nobility,

H                           and

and as bufie to encroch upon their Marches, and add more to his own limited Soveraignty, as they were to draw down thofe few prerogatives it had, into that well mixt, and ballanced *Ariftocracie* of theirs.

*Denmark*, howfoever by the opportunity, and narrowneſs of his Sound, reftrained to the felfneſs of profit; yet by difcipline, and feat, able to fecond an active undertaker with fhipping, money, &c. But too wife, with thefe ftrengths to help any forrain Prince to become Emperor over himfelf, or otherwife to entangle his Eftate offenfively, or defenfively in common Actions.

The *Sweden* environed, or rather imprifoned with great and dangerous neighbours, and enemies. The *Polae* pretending Title to his Kingdom, and with a continuall claim by fword, inforceing him to a perpetuall defenfive charge. The King of *Denmark* being unfafe to him upon

on every occafion, by ill neighbour-
hood among active Princes. And
laftly,the barbarous *Mofcovite*, onely
quiet through his own diftreffe, and
oppreffions elfe-where. So as like a
Prince thus ftrictly invironed, the
King of *Sweden* could not (among
Princes )ftand as any pregnant place
of exorbitant help, or terror;other-
wife than by money.

The *Switzers* fwoln with equality;
divided at home; enemies, yet fervants to Monarchies; not eafily oppreffed, in the opinion of thofe
times; nor able to doe any thing of
note alone: and fo a dangerous body
for the foul of *Spanie* to infufe defignes into.

The Princes of *Italy* carefull to
bind one another by common caution; reftrained from the freedom of
their own counfells, by force of
ftronger powers above them, and as
bufie in keeping down their people,
to multiply profit out of them, as to

entife

entife the ftranger thither, to gain moderately by him. Through which narrow kind of wifdom, they being become rather Merchant than Monarchall States, were confined from challenging their own, or enlarging their dominions upon neighbors;and laftly, in afpect to other Princes rights, conjured within neutrall Circles, by the myfticall practife of an abufing *Conclave*, and afpiring Monarch of *Spain*.

The *Mofcovite* bridled by his barbarous neighbor the *Tartar* ; and through natural ignorance, and incivility,like a poor Tenant upon a rich Farm, unequall to his inferiors.

The *Grand Signior* afleep in his *Saraglia* ; as having turned the ambition of that growing Monarchy into idle luft ; corrupted his Martiall difcipline; prophaned his *Alcoran*, in making war againft his own Church, and not in perfon, but by his *Bafha's* ; confequently by all apparance, declining

clining into his people by such, but
more precipitate degrees, as his active
Anceftors had climbed above them.

Now while all thefe Princes lived
thus fettered within the narrownefs
of their own Eftates, or humors;
*Spain* managing the *Popedome* by voices, and penfions among the Cardi-
nals, and having the fword both by
land, & fea in his hand; feemed likewife to have all thofe Weftern-parts
of the world, laid as a *Tabula rafa* before him, to write where he pleafed;
*To el Ré.* And that which made this
fatal profpect the more probable, was
his golden Indian Mines; kept open,
not only to feed, and carry his threatning Fleets, & Armies, where he had
will, or right to goe; but to make
way, and pretenfe for more, where he
lift, by corrupting, and terrifying the
chief Counfels both of Chriftian and
Heathen Princes. Which tempting,
and undermining courfe had already
given fuch reputation both to his Ci-

vill

vill and Martiall actions; that he was even then grown as impossible to please, as dangerous to offend.

And out of which fearfull Almanack this wakeful Patriot, besides an universall terror upon all Princes, saw ( as I said ) that this immense power of *Spain* did cast a more particular aspect of danger upon his native Countrey : and such as was not likely to be prevented, or secured by any other Antidote, than a generall league among free Princes, to undertake this undertaker at home. To make this course plausible, though he knew the Qu. of *England* had already engaged her fortunes into it, by protecting the States Generall, yet perceiving her Governours ( as I said ) to sit at home in their soft chairs, playing fast or loose with them that ventured their lives abroad ; he providently determined that while *Spain* had peace, a Pope, money, or credit; and the world men, necessity,

or

or humors; the war could hardly be determined upon this Low-Countrey ftage.

Becaufe if the neighbour-hood of *Flanders,* with help of the fuddain fea paffage, fhould tempt thefe united Princes to fall upon that limb of the *Spaniſh* Empire; it would prove (as he fuppofed) an affailing of him in the ftrongeft feat of his war; where all exchanges, paffages, and fupplies were already fetled to his beft advantage: and fo a force bent againſt him, even where himfelf could wiſh it.

*Flanders* being a Province repleniſhed with offenfive, and defenfive Armies: and fortified with divers ftrong Cities: of which the affailing Armies muft be conftrained, either to leave many behind them, or elfe to hazard the lofs of time, and their gallanteft Troops in befieging of one.

Again he conceived that *France* it felf was like enough to be tender, in

fecr u-
p

seconding our defignes with horfe,or
foot there ; our neighbour-hood upon the fame Continent ( out of old
acquaintance ) not being over-wel-
come to them,as he prefumed. And
for fuccors from other Princes ; they
were to come far, and pafs through
divers dominions with difficulty, diftraction,lofs of time, and perchance
loofe-handed difcipline.

And fo concludes, firft, that it
would be hard for us to become abfolute Mafters of the field in *Flanders,*
or to ground our affailing of him
there upon any other argument,than
that ever-betraying *Fallax* of under-
valuing our enemies, or fetling undertaking Counfels upon market-
mens Intelligence, as *Cæfar* faith the
*French* in his time ufed to do. Which
confident wayes, without any curious examination what power the adverfe party hath prepared to encounter, by defenfe, invafion, or divifion muft probably make us lofers,
                                   oth

both in men, money, and reputation.
And upon thefe and the like affump-
fits he refolved, there were but two
ways left to fruftrate this ambitious
Monarchs defignes. The one, that
which diverted *Hanibal*, and by fet-
ting fire on his own houfe made him
draw in his Spirits to comfort his
heart; the other that of *Iafon* by
fetching away his golden Fleece, and
not fuffering any one man quietly to
enjoy that, which every man fo
much affected.

✤✤✤✤✤✤✤✤✤✤✤✤✤✤✤✤✤✤✤✤✤

## CHAP. IX.

TO carry war into the bowels of
*Spain*, and by the affiftance of
the *Netherlands*, burn his fhipping in
all havens as they paffed along; and
in that paffage furprize fome well-
chofen place for wealth, & ftrength :
eafie to be taken, and poffiible to be
kept

kept by us : he ſuppoſed to be the ſafeſt, moſt quick, and honourable Counſell of diverſion. Becauſe the ſame ſtrength of ſhipping which was offenſively imployed to carry forces thither; and by the way to interrupt all Martiall preparations, and proviſions of that griping ſtate ; might by the convenient diſtance between his Coaſt, & ours (if the *Spaniard* ſhould affect to pay us with our own monies ) fitly be diſpoſed both wayes ; and ſo like two arms of a naturall body (with little addition of charge ) defend, and offend ; ſpend and ſupply at one time.

Or, if we found our own ſtock, or neighbours contribution ſtrong enough to follow good ſucceſs to greater deſignes ; then whether our adventure once more, in ſtirring up ſpirit in the *Portugall* againſt the *Caſtilians* tyranny over them, were not to caſt a chance for the beſt part of his wealth, reputation, & ſtrength, both of

of men and shipping in all his dominions.

Again, left the pride of *Spain* should
be secretly ordain'd to scourge it self,
for having been a scourge to so many, and yet in this reall inquisition e-
scape the audacity of undertaking
Princes; Sir *Philip* thought fit to put
the world in mind, that *Sevill* was a
fair City; secure in a rich soyl, and
plentiful traffique; but an effeminate
kind of people, guarded with a conquering name; and consequently a
fair bait to the piercing eyes of ambitious Generals, needy Souldiers, and
greedy Mariners. In like sort hee
mentioned *Cales*, as a strength, and
key to her traffiquefull, & navigable
river, not fit to be neglected in such
a defensive, and diverting enterprise,
but at least to be examined.

Laftly, whether this audacity of
undertaking the conqueror at home;
would not, with any moderate suc-
cefs, raise up a new face of things in
thofe

thofe parts ; and fuddainly ftir up
many fpirits, to move againſt the
fame power, under which they long
have bin ſlaviſhly conjur'd,& by this
affront,prove a deforming blemiſh in
the nice fortune of a fearfull uſurper?
    Or if that ſhall be thought an un-
dertaking too full of charge, hazard,
or difficulty; then whether it wil not
be juſt in the wiſdome of Eftate, ma-
naged among active Princes ; that as
Qu. *Elizabeth* had ever been tender,
in preſerving her Soveraignty upon
the narrow ſeas ; and wiſely conſide-
red, how nature, to maintain that
birth-right of hers,had made all wars
by ſea far more cheap, proper, and
commodious to her, than any expedition upon land could poſſibly be:I
ſay, whether to continue this claim,
would not prove honour to her ſelf,
advantage to her traffique,and reputation to her people ; I mean, if ſhee
ſhould pleaſe, in thoſe cloudy humors, & queſtions reigning between
                              her

her felf, and other Princes, to keep a
ftrong fucceffive fleet, all feafonable
times of the year, upon this pretty
*Sleeve*, or *Ocean* of hers? I fay, to keep
them as provident furveyers what
did paffe from one ftate to another,
wherein the law of Nature, or Nations had formerly given her intereft
to an offenfive, or defenfive fecurity.
A Regall inquifition, and worthy of
a fea-Soveraign, without wronging
friends, or neighbours, to have a perfect intelligence what they had, or
wanted for delicacy, peace, or war in
generall: And in particular, a clear
perfpective glafs into her enemies
Merchant, or Martiall traffique, ena-
bling this Queen fo to ballance this
ambitious *Leviathan* in either kind;
as the little fifhes, his fellow Citizens,
might travell, multiply, & live quietly by him under the protecton of nature.

Again, let us confider, whether out
of this, or the like Audit, it will not
be

be found a juft tribute to opportunity, the rudder of all ftate wifedoms.
That as Qu. *Elizabeth* was a Soveraign, which refted with her fex at
home, and yet moved all fexes a-
broad to their own good;whether (I
fay) as fhe from a devoted zeal to the
Church,had by Sir *Nich.Throgmorton*,
in the beginning of her reign,ftirred
up fpirits in that over-mitred *French*
Kingdom,to become watchful guar-
dians of peace, and Religion there.
I fay, whether in the fame Chriftian
providence there might not, by the
neglect, or breach of many Treaties,
an occafion be juftly taken to reap a
reafonable harveft out of that well-
chofen feed time,by receiving *Rochel*,
*Breft*, *Bourdeaux*, or any other place
upon that Continent, diftreffed for
Religion, into her abfolute protection? Neverthelefs, not with intent of
reconquering any part of her ancient
Domanies, lineally defcended from
many anceftors ; howfoever thofe
places

places fo taken may feem feated like
tempters of Princes, to plead in the
Court of *Mars* fuch native , though
difcontinued rights, as no time can
prefcribe againft; but only to keep
thofe humble religious fouls free
from oppreffion, in that fuper-Jefui-
ted foveraignty.

In which religious defigne to encourage the Qu. he advifed us to examine *if* the diverfions naturally rifing amongft their unlimited *French
Grandees,* grown up *per faltum* with
their Kings above Laws, Parliaments,
and Peoples freedom; would not in
all probability caft up fom light duft
into their fuperiors eys, as tributes to
their common Idol *Difcorder*; and fo
perchance either by treaty, or fight of
the firft Army, ftir up *Bouillon,* & *Ro-
han* for Religion; other Roytelets
w^th hope to make fafe their fubaltern
governments, even through the ruines of that over-foring foveraignty?

And is not as probable again, that
even

even the greateft Cities, raifed and
ftanding upon the like waving en-
croachments of time, & advantagious power would readily become
jealous of the leaft ftrict hand carried
over them, by interruption of traffique, greedinefs of Governors, pride
of their own wealth, or indefinite
impofitions; as *Paris*, *Bourdeaux*, *Mar-
feilles*, *Roan*, or *Lyons*? whereby they
might likewife be tempted, either to
run head-long with the ftream, or at
the leaft to ftand at gaze, and leave
the Heraldry of Princes to be decided by the ftronger party, as for the
moft part, they hitherto have been.

Nay in this Climax to come nearer
yet; is it probable that even the Catholique Princes, and Provinces en-
vironing this vaft Kingdome, would
(as now they doe) for want of vent,
break their hopes, and fervilly run
out upon the ground like water, and
not rather when this new rent fhould
appear, chufe to fhake off a charge-
                                    able,

able, & fervile yoke of Mountebank
holinefs under *Spanifh Rome*, and to
that end prefently mingle money,
counfels, and forces with ours? As
quickly refolved that this way of a
ballancing union, amongft abfolute
Princes, would prove quieter reft for
them, and founder foundations for
us, than our former parties did, when
we conquered *France*, more by fuch
factious & ambitious affiftances, than
by any odds of our Bows, or Beef-ea-
ters, as the *French* were then fcornfully pleas'd to terme us : I fay, even
when in the pride of our conquefts,
we ftrove to gripe more than was
poffible for us to hold; as appears by
our being forced to come away, and
leave our anceftors bloud, and bones
behind, for Monuments not of enjoy-
ing, but of over-griping & expulfion.
  So that the fum of all is ; whether
the taking or furprize of *Cales, Rochel,
Bourdeaux,* or fome fuch other good
out, or inlet upon that Mayn, offered,
into our protection, would not prove

I                    honour

honour to us, as a brave earneſt either to war, or peace? Beneficiall to the *French* King, and Crown againſt their wills; as manifeſting to their hot ſpirits, and young Councels, that undertaking is not all? And beſides clearly ſhewing, in *Mars* his true glaſs, how that once wel-formed Monarchy had by little, and little, let fal her ancient, and reverend pillars, (I mean Parliaments, Lawes, and Cuſtomes) into the narrowneſs of Proclamations, or Imperiall Mandates : by which like baſtard children of tyranny ſhe hath transformed her Gentry into Peaſants, her Peaſants into ſlaves, Magiſtracy into Sale works, Crown-revenue into Impoſitions. And therein likewiſe publiſhed the differences between Monarchs, and Tyrants ſo clearly to the world, as hereafter all Eſtates, that would take upon their necks the yoke of Tyranny, muſt juſtly be reputed voluntary ſlaves in the choice of that paſſive bondage.

Whereby, one queſtion naturally beget-

begetting another, the next ( as I
take it ) muſt be what this Auſtrian
aſpiring familie would doe, while
theſe two Kingdoms ſhould ſtand
thus engaged? Whether invade the
King of *Denmark* alone, hoping by his
ruine to ſubdue the yet ſubdued
Princes of *Germany* to get the Sound,
and Eaſtern Seas, with all their Maritime riches into his power : to
bring the Hanſe Towns into ſome
captivated ſubjections, and thereby
become Soveraign over all *Eaſtern*
traffique by Sea, and land? Or elſe by
lulling *France* aſleep with Imperiall
Matches, or promiſes, finde means
to ſteal the Flower-de-luce into the
Lyons garland ; and in that currant
of proſperity to Citadellize the
long oppreſſed *Netherlands* into a tenure of uttermoſt bondage ; and ſo
build up his Eagles neſt above the
threatning of any inferior Region.

But it many times pleaſeth God by
the breaking out of concealed flaſh-
es from theſe fatall cloudes of craft,

or

or violence, to awake even the moſt
ſuperſtitious Princes out of their en-
chanted dreams; and cauſe them
to reſiſt ſuddainly to make head a-
gainſt this devouring *Sultan*, with
leagues offenſive, and defenſive;And
by an unexpected union to become
ſuch frontier neighbours to this
Crown-hunter, as he might with
great reaſon doubt their trading upon his large cloven feet, who intended to have ſet them ſo heavily upon the heads of many more ancient
States, Peoples, or Scepters than his
own. And laſtly, in the ſame preſs,
by this one affront in the Lions face,
publiſhing to the world that power
is infinite no where but in God.: ſo
as the firſt blow well ſtricken, moſt
commonly ſucceeds with honor,
and advantage to the judicious, able,
and active undertakers.

Out of which divine providence,
governing all ſecond cauſes by the
firſt, is it not probable that even the
naturall viciſſitudes of war, and
peace,

peace, would bring forth fome active
propofitions between thefe many
waies allied Kingdomes of *England*,
and *France*, to a perfect reconciliation, and as many again of irreconci-
liable divifion between them, and
*Spain*? *France* being ftirred up by a
joint counfell,. and propofition of
affiftance, to the recovery of her long
fleeping rights in *Navarre*, or *Naples*;
and *England* onely to diftract this
ambitious Monarch from his late
Cuftom, in depofing Kings, and
Princes, as *Navarre, Portugall*, the
*Palatine, Brunfwick*, and &c. as in a fecond courfe of his devouring glutto-
ny, interrupt him from future pro-
fecutions of *Denmark*, and *Germany*
it felf, to the fame end; with his conftant intent, to bring all the earth
under one mans tyranny.

To prevent which deluge of bound-
lefs power, Sir *Philip* was of opinion,
that more than charge, it could be no
prejudice ; if to the unvizarding of
this masked triplicity between

I 3  *Spain*

*Spain*, *Rome* and the Soveraign Iefuits of *France*; I fay if the *Queen*, as de-
fendrefs of the faith, for a main pledg
of this new offenfive, and defenfive
undertaken league, would be pleafed to affift the French King with the
fame forces by Sea, or land, wherewith, till then, fhe had juftly oppofed
againft him. And confequently put-
ing the Spaniard from an offenfive,
to a defenfive War, manifeftly publifh, and give credit to this unbelie-
ved truth, *viz.* that this Arch-Con-
queror never intended other favor
to the Pope, Emperor, or Iefuits, in
all this conjunction, than *Poliphemus*
promifed to *Ulyffes*, which was, that
they fhould be the laft whom he
purpofed to devour.

And farther to encourage thefe
great Princes in this true balancing
defigne with the chargeable, and
thorny paffages proper to it; he providently faw the long threatned
Dutchie of *Savoy* would be in their
view; with affurance that this active
Prince

Prince would think it a fafe diverfi-
fion of dangers from his domeſticall
Eſtate, and a fit ſtage to act his forrain cobwebbs upon, if he might
have them ſhadowed under the
wings of ſtronger, and every way
more able Powers; without which
his mean Eſtate muſt in all probability force him to ſhift his outward
garments perchance too often.

The *Venetians* again, foreſeeing with
their Ariſtocraticall jealouſie, that
their Eſtate had onely two pregnant
dangers hanging over it; the one
Eaſtward from the grand Signior,
who eaſily moves not his encom-
paſſing half Moon; the other Weſt-
ward from this *Solyman* of *Spain*,
whoſe unſatiable ambition, they
knew, would reſt upon no centre, but
creep along the Mediterranean Seas,
till he might (contrary to the nature
of thoſe waters) over-flow all weak;
or ſecure neighbor Princes, without
any other title, or quarrell, than *Stet
pro ratione voluntas.* And foreſeeing a-

I 4 gain

gain in this suddain violence, that they
could expect no Estate to be selfly
engaged in their succor; but must resolve to stand, or fall alone by that
course. Where, on the other side, if
the Eastern half-Moon should but
seem to move towards them , they
were assured to have all the Estates
of *Europe*, engaged by their own interests, to joine with them. Upon
this view there is no doubt, but that
wise City would have resolved it to
be a choice of less evill, to joine with
these great Princes , in diverting his
Spanish gallies, and galleons by Sea,
and his inveterate Armies by land
from disturbing, or subjecting the
safety, and traffique of all Christen-
dom to his seven patch'd coated
Kingdomes, rather than for want of
heart or opportunity, to stand neuter
( as they doe) and become treasurers
both of money, and munition for
him, that already intends thus to
conquer them, and enjoy it.

Again, shall we ( said Sir *Philip*) in
thefe

thefe colleftions of particulars, forget the State of *Italy* it felf? which
excellent temper of fpirits, earth, and
aire, having long been fmothered,
and mowed down by the differing
Tyrannies of *Spain*, and *Rome*, fhall
we not be confident they would, upon the approaching of thefe armies,
both ftir up thofe benumbed Soveraignties, which onely bear the name
of free Princes, to affeft their own
Manumiffions, & help to chafe away
thefe fucceeding and oppreffing
Garrifons, whofe fore-fathers for many yeares had fold life, libertie, and
lawes for eight pence the day; and fo
refolutely oppofe thofe Spanifh-
born, or Spanifh-fworn Tyrannies,
which have for divers ages Lorded
over that moft equally tempered
Nation.

Or whether the winter in thofe
Seas, giving opportunity without
fufpition, may not encourage the
Claim of our old rights in the Kingdom of *Sicilie*, more legall than moft
of

of his Spanish intrufions; and therein be welcome to the Grand Signior,
the freedom of *Algiers*, even to *Italy*
it felf. And befides, if we profpered,
yield abundance of wealth by fpoil,
and trade : with fuch a feat for di-
verfion, or poffeffion, as by many vi-
fible, and invifible. helps, might be
kept, or put away with infinite advantage?

Laftly, he made a Quære, whether
the Pope himfelf would not (like a
fecular Prophet )to keep his becoming Chaplain a little the farther off;
either wink, or at leaft delay his
thundering curfes, or fupplies of *Pe-
ter-pence* againft thefe qualifying Armies, onely to moderate the over-
greatneffe of his Spanifh Monarchie?
whofe infancie having been nourifhed under the Miters holy water, and
fophiftries of his practifing *Conclaves*,
dares now imperioufly publifh to
the world a refolution, of taking all
other diftinctions from amongft
men, faving that Canonicall regiment

ment of wit and might, whereby he
might fo preferve his fpirituall ambition entire, without any charge or
change of Religion, or Soveraignties
from one hand to another, but like a
holy father mediate the reftoring of
*Italy* to her ancient free, and diftinct
Principalities. Whereby now by this
moderate courfe, admit the Pope for
his part, fhould impair his temporall
profits, and fubaltern jurisdiction a
while; yet fhall he be fure, ( as I faid)
to multiply his fpirituall honors, and
inlarge that Kingdom , by thefe
works of *Supererogation.* And by
joyning with his fellow Princes in a
contribution, by way of accompt, or
countenance to pay thefe great Armies, be fure to fit rent-free under
his, and their own vines, as abfolute
fpirituall, and temporall Princes
ought to doe?

From which ( faith he ) this con-
clufion will probably follow; that
the undertaking of this *Antonie* fingle, I mean *France*, would prove a
begetting

begetting of brave occafions jointly to difturb this Spanifh *Ottoman*, in all his waies of crafty, or forcible conquefts. Efpecially fince *Queen Elizabeth*, the ftandard of this conjunction, would infallibly incline to unite with the better part, and by a fuddain changing of *Mars* his Imperious Enfignes, into a well ballanced treaty of univerfall Peace, reftore and keep the world within her old *equilibrium* or bounds.

And the rather, becaufe her long cuftom in governing, would quickly have made her difcern, that it had been impoffible, by force, or any human wifdom to have qualified thefe over-grown Combinations of *Spain*; but onely by a countermining of party with party, and a diftracting of exorbitant defires, by cafting a gray-headed cloud of fear over them; thereby manifefting the well difguifed yokes of bondage, under which our Modern Conquerors would craftily entice the Nown-adjective-

jective-natured Princes, and subjects
of this time to submit their necks. A
map ( as it pleafed her to fay ) of his
fecrets, in which fhe confeffed herfelf to be the more ripe, becaufe under the like falfe Enfignes, though
perchance better mafked, fhe had
feen *Philip* the fecond after the fame
meafure, or with little difference, to
*Henry* the third of *France*, a principall fellow-member in that earthly
founded, though heavenly feeming
Church of *Rome*, when he redelivered
*Amiers*, *A: beville*, &c. together with
that fouldier-like paffage made by
the Duke of *Parma* through *France*,
to the relief of *Paris*; yet whether this
provident *Philip* did frame thefe fpecious charities of a conqueror, *Au-
guftus*-like, afpiring to live after
death greater than his fucceffor; or
providently forefeeing that the divers humors in fucceeding Princes,
would prove unable to maintain
fuch green ufurpations, in the heart
of a Kingdom competitor with his

seven-headed *Hydra* kept together
onely by a constant ard unnaturall
wheel of fortune, till some new
child of hers, like *Henry* the fourth,
should take his turn in restoring all
unjust combinations or encrochments; or lastly, whether, like a true
cutter of Cumine seedes, he did not
craftily lay these hypocritall sacrifices upon theAltar of death,as peace-
offerings from pride to the temple
of fear, as smoaks dying of a disea-
sed conscience choked up with innocent bloud: of all which perplexed
pedigrees, I know not what to determine otherwise; than that these
Tyrannicall enchrochments doe carry the images of Hell, and her thunder-workers, in their own breasts,as
fortune doth misfortunes in that
wind-blown,vast,and various womb
of hers.

Or if this should seem of too high
a nature, or too many chargeable
parts : then whether to begin again
where we left    and by the example
of

of *Drake*, a mean born fubject to the
Crown of *England*, invade, poffefs, &
nhabite fome well chofen havens in
*Peru*, *Mexico*, or both, were not to
ftrike at the root, & affail him where
he is weakeft; & yet gathers his chie-
feft ftrength to make himfelf Monarch over all the Weftern Climes?
fupplyes being as eafie to us, as to
him, we having both winds, and feas
indifferently open between us.

❧✿❧✿❧✿❧✿❧✿❧✿❧✿❧✿❧✿❧✿❧✿❧✿❧✿

## CHAP. X.

UPon due confideration of which
particulars, he fore-feeing that
each of the former required greater
refolution, union, and expenfe, than
the naturality, diffidence, and quiet
complexion of the Princes then reigning could well bear; and befides the
freedome of choyce to bee taken a-
way, or at the leaft obftructed by fatall mifts of ignorance, or factious
counfells reigning among the Minifters of Kings: he refolved from the
only

grounds of his former intended voiage with Sir *Francis Drake*, that the only credible means left, was, to affail him by invafion, or incurfion ( as occafion fell out)in fome part of that rich, and defert Weft-Indian Mine.

Firft, becaufe it is an obfervation among the wifeft, that as no man is a Prophet in his own Countrey ; fo all men may get honour much cheaper far off than at home, and at fea more eafily than at land.

Secondly, in refpect he difcovered the Spanifh conquefts in thofe remote parts, fo much noifed throughout the world, to be indeed like their Jefuits Miracles; which comming far, were multiplied by Fame and Art, to keep other Nation sin wonder, and blind worfhip.

Thirdly, out of confident beliefe, that their inhumane cruelties had fo difpeopled, & difpleafed thofe countreys ; that as he was fure to find no great power to withftand him ; fo might he well hope the Reliques of
thofe

thofe oppreffed *Cimerons* would joy-
fully take Arms with any forrainer
to redeem their liberty, and revenge
their parents bloud.

Fourthly, by reafon the fcale of diftance between *Spain* & *America* was
fo great; as it infallibly affured Sir
*Philip* he fhould find leafure enough
to land, fortifie, and become Maiter
of the field, before any fuccour could
come thither to interrupt him.

Fiftly, the pride, delicacy, and fecurity of the *Spaniard*, which made him
live without Difcipline; and truft
more to the greatnefs of his name a-
broad, than any ftrength, order, courage, or munition at home.

Sixtly, Sir *Philip* prophecying what
the pedigrees of Princes did warrant,
I mean the happy conjunction of
of *Scotland*, to thefe populous Realms
*England* & *Ireland*; forefaw, that if
this multitude of people were not
ftudioufly husbanded, and difpofed,
they would rather diminifh, than
add any ftrength to this Monarchy.

K　　　　Which

Which danger (he conjectured) could only by this designe of forrain imploiment, or the peaceable harvest of manufactures at home, be safely prevented.

The seventh, and a chief motive indeed was, that no other action could be less subject to emulation of Court, less straining to the present humors of State, more concurring with expectation, and voice of time; nor wherein there was greater possibility of improving merit, wealth, & friends.

Lastly, he did, as all undertakers must doe, believe that there is ever good intelligence between chance & hazard, and so left some things not summed up before hand by exact minutes. But rather thought good to venture upon the cast of a *Rubicon* Dy; either to stop his springs of gold, and so drie up that torrent which carried his subduing Armies every where; or else by the wakefull providence of threatned neighbors, force him to waft home that conquering

Metall

Metall with infinite charge, and not-
withstanding unwarranted from enriching those enemies, whom he prin-
cipally studied to suppress by it.

To confirm which opinion, he foresaw how this racked vanity of the
*Spanish* government ( intending to
work a change in the free course
of nature) had interdicted all manufacture, traffick, or vent by sea, or
land, between the natives of *Ameri-*
*ca*, & all nations else, *Spain* excepted.
And withall, to make the barrenness
of *Spain* more fertile, how he had im-
proved that idle *Castilian*, by imployments, in activeness, wealth, and authority over those vanquished creatures; suffering the poor native *Ame-*
*ricans* to be suppreft with heavy impositions, discouraging idleness, bondage of laws, sheering of the humble
sheep to cloath the proud devouring
Wolves; finally, under these, & such
like quintessences of tyranny striving
( as I said ) even besides nature, to
make barren *Spain* the Monarchy, &

K 2 that

that every way more fertile *America*
to be the Province. All which affections of power to be wiſer, & ſtronger
than the truth, this Gentleman concluded would in fulnes of time make
manifeſt; that the heavy can no more
be forced to aſcend, and reſt fixed
there, than the light to goe down-
ward, as to their proper center.

Notwithſtanding, the ſtate of Tyrants is ſo ſublime, and their errors
founded upon ſuch precipitate ſteps,
as this growing *Spaniard* both did,
doth, and ever will travell ( with his
forefathers in Paradiſe) to be equall,
or above his Maker; and ſo to impri-
ſon divine laws within the narrownes
of will, and humane wiſdome, with
the fettred ſelfsneſſes of cowardly or
other confident Tyranny. In which
prepoſterous courſes, to prevent all
poſſibility of commotion, let the
Reader be pleaſed to obſerve; how
that continually he forceth his
own ſubjects free-denized in *Ameri-*
*ca*, to fetch weapons of defence, con-
queſt,

queft, invafion ; as well as ornament,
wealth, neceffity, and delicacy, out of
*spain*, meerly to retain want, fupply,
price, weight, fafhion, and meafure,
ftill (contrary to nature)in that barren Crown of *Caftile*, with an abfolute power refting in himfelf to
rock, or eafe both peoples, according
to the waving ends of an unfteddy,
and fharp pointed Pyramis of power.

Nay, to rife yet a ftep higher in this
bloudy pride; Sir *Philip*, our unbelie-
ved *Caffandra*, obferved this limit-
lefs ambition of the *Spaniard* to have
chofen that uttermoft Citadell of
bondage, I mean the Inquifition
of *spain*, for her inftrument. Not, as
in former Masks, to prune, or govern;
but in a confidence rifing out of the
old age of fuperftitious fantafms, utterly to root out all feeds of humane
freedom; and (as Sr *Philip* conceived)
with fatal diffolution to it felf. In refpect that thefe types of extremity
would foon publifh to the world,
what little difference Tyrants ftrive

to leave between the creation, ufe, and honor of men, and beafts, valuing them indifferently but as Counters, to fum up the divers, nay contrary ufes,and Audits of fublime and wandring fupremacy, which true glafs would(in this Gentlemans opinion) fhew the moft dull & cowardly eye, that Tyrants be not nurfing Fathers, but ftep-fathers; and fo no anointed deputies of God,but rather lively Images of the dark Prince,that fole author of dif-creation, and diforder, who ever ruines his ends with over-building.

Laftly, where his reafon ended, there many divine Precepts, and Examples did affure him, that the vengeance of God muft neceffarily hang over thofe hypocriticall cruelties, which under colour of converting fouls to him, fent millions of better than their own, they cared not whither:And in ftead of fpreading Chriftian religion by good life, committed fuch terrible inhumanities, as

gave

gave thofe that lived under nature
manifeft occafion to abhor the devi-
ly characters of fo tyrannical a deity.
   Now though this juftice of the Al-
mighty be many times flow,& therefore neglected here on earth ; yet ( I
fay) under the only conduct of this
ftar did Sir *Philip* intend to revive
this hazardous enterprize of Plant-
ing upon the Main of *America*; projected, nay undertaken long before,
(as I fhewed you) but ill executed in
the abfence of Sir *Philip* ; with a defigne to poffefs *Nombre de Dios* , or
fome other haven near unto it , as
places, in refpect of the little diftance
between the two feas, efteemed the
fitteft *Rendez-vouz* for fupply, or retreat of an Army upon all occafions.
And befides , by that means to circle
in his wealth and freedome, with a
joynt fore-running Fleet; to the end,
that if the fortune of Conqueft profpered not with them, yet he fhould
infallibly pay the charge of both Navies, with infinite lofs, and dif-repu-
tation to the *Spaniard.*        And

And in this project Sir *Philip* proceeded so far with the united Provinces, as they yeelded to assist, and second the ships of his Soveraign, under his charge, with a fleet of their own. Which, besides a present addition of strength, he knew would lead in others by example.

Again, for supply of these Armies, he had ( out of that naturall tribute, which all free spirits acknowledge to superior worth ) won 30 Gentlemen of great bloud, and state here in *England*, every man to sell one hundred pounds land, to second, and countenance this first Fleet with a stronger.

Now when these beginnings were by his own credit and industrie thus well setled: then to give an excellent form to a reall work, hee contrived this new intended Plantation, not like an *Assylum* for fugitives, a *Bellum Piraticum* for *Banditi*, or any such base *Ramas* of people; but as an *Emporium* for the confluence of all Nations that love, or profess any kind kinde of vertue , or Commerce.

Wherein to incite thofe that tarried at home to adventure, he propounded the hope of a fure, and rich return. To Martiall men he opened wide the door of fea and land, for fame and conqueft. To the nobly ambitious the far ftage of *America,* to win honour in. To the Religious divines, befides a new Apoftolicall calling of the laft heathen to the Chriftian faith, a large field of reducing poor Chriftians, mif-led by the Idolatry of *Rome,* to their mother *Primitive* Church. To the ingenuoufly induftrious variety of natural richeffes, for new myfteries, and manufactures to work upon. To the Merchant , with a fimple people, a fertile, and unexhaufted earth. To the fortunebound, liberty. To the curious, a. fruitfull womb of innovation. Generally the word gold was an attractive Adamant, to make men venture that which they have , in hope to grow rich by that which they have not.                                   What

What the expectation of this voyage was, the time paſt can beſt witnes; but what the ſucceſs ſhould have been (till it be revived by ſome ſuch generous undertakers ) lies hid in Gods ſecret judgements, who did at once cut off this Gentlemans life, and ſo much of our hope.

Upon theſe enterpriſes of his, I have preſumed to ſtand the longer, becauſe from the aſhes of this firſt propounded voyage to *America*, that fatall *Low Country* action ſprang up, in which this worthy Gentleman loſt his life. Beſides, I do ingenuouſly confeſs, that it delights me to keep company with him, even after death ; eſteeming his actions, words, and converſation, the daintieſt treaſure my mind could then lay up ; or can at this day impart with our poſteritie.

✦✧✦✧✦✧✦✧✦✧✦✧✦✧✦✧✦✧✦✧✦✧✦✧✦✧

## *C H A P. XI.*

THerefore to come at the laſt to that diverting imployment,

promifed to him under hisUncle in
the Low-Countries: he was, upon
his return to the Court, inftantly
made for Garrifon, Governor of *Flu-
fhing*,and for the Field,General of the
Horfe;in both which charges,his car-
riage teftified to the world,wifdome,
and valour, with addition of honour
to his Country by them.

For inftance; how like a Souldier
did he behave himfelf,firft in contri-
ving, then in executing the furprife
of *Axil*? where he revived that ancient, and fecure difcipline of order,&
filence in their March;and after their
entrance into the town,placed a band
of choice fouldiers to make a ftand
in the Market-place, for fecuritie to
the reft, that were forced to wander
up and down by direction of Commanders; and when the fervice was
done, rewarded that obedience of
difcipline in every one, liberally,out
of his own purfe.

How providently again did he preferve the lives and honor of our En-
gllfh

glish Army, at that enterprise of *Gravelin?* where though he was guided by directions given him; yet whether out of arguments drawn from the person of *La Motte,* Commander of that town, who had a generall reputation of too much worth, either *Simon*-like to deceive, or easily to be deceived; or out of the strength and importance of that place, precious to the owner in many respects, the least of which would redouble loss to the growing ambition of a Conqueror; or whether upon caution given by intelligence; or whatsoever light of diversion else; he (I say) was resolute not to hazzard so many principall Gentlemen, with such gallant Troops and Commanders which accompanied him, in that flattering expedition. Yet because he kept this steady counsel in his own bosome, there was labouring on every side to obtain the honour of that service. To all which gallant kind of competition, he made this answer, that his own comming

thither

.hither was to the fame end, wherein
.hey were now become his rivalls; &
therfore affured them, that he would
not yeeld any thing to any man,
which by right of his place was both
due to himfelf, and confequently difgrace for him to execute by others:
again, that by the fame rule, he would
never confent to hazzard them that
were his friends, and in divers re-
fpects his equalls, where he found
reafon to make many doubts, and fo
little reafon to venture himfelf.

Yet as a Commander, concluding
fomething fit to be done, equally for
obedience and triall, he made the inferior fort of Captains try their fortune by dice upon a drums head: the
lot fell upon Sir *William Brown* his
own Lieutenant, who with a choice
company prefently departed, receiving this provifionall caution from
Sir *Philip*, that if he found practife,
& not faith, he fhould ftreight throw
down his Arms, and yeeld himfelf
prifoner; protefting that if they took
him,

him, he fhould be ranfomed ; if they broke quarter, his death moft feverely revenged.

On thefe forlorn companies go with this Leader, & before they came into the town, found all outward fignals exactly performed ; when they were entred, every ftreet fafe and quiet, according to promife, till they were paft any eafie recovery of the gate; then inftantly out of the cellars under ground, they were charged by Horfe and Foot. The Leader, following his Generalls commandement, difcovers the treafon, throws down his arms, and is taken prifoner. The reft of the company retire, or rather fly towards their fhips, but ftil wounded and cut off by purfuit of their enemies ; till at length a Serjeant of a band, with fifteen more, all *sidney's* men (I mean fuch as could die to win honour, and do fervice to their country) made a halt, and being fortunately mixt of pikes, halberds, and mufkets, refolved to be flain with their

backs

backs to their friends, and their faces
to their enemies; they moved, or ftai-
ed with occafion ; and were in both
continually charged with Foot and
Horfe, till in the end eight were flain,
and eight left alive. With thefe the
Serjeant wounded at the fide with a
fquare die out of a field-piece, made
this brave retreat within view and at
laft protection of their own Navy;
oringing home even in the wounds ,
nay ruins of himfelf, and company,
reputation of courage, and Martiall
difcipline to his Country.

Moreover, in thofe private acci-
dents of difcontentment & quarrell ,
which naturally accompany great
fpirits in the beft governed Camps ,
how difcreetly did Sir *Philip* ballance
that brave *Hollock,* made head of a
party againft his Uncle ? When put-
ing himfelf between indignities offered to his Soveraign, through the
Earl of *Leicefters* perfon ; and yet not
fit for a fupreme Governors place to
ground a duel upon ; he brought
                                    thofe

thofe paffionate charges, which the Count *Hollock* addreffed upwards to the Earl, down by degrees upon himfelf. Where that brave Count *Hollock* found Sir *Philip* fo fortified with wifdom, courage, and truth ; befides the ftrong partie of former friend-fhip ftanding for him in the Counts noble nature ; as though fenfe of honour, and many things elfe equal, and unequal between them, were in apparance beyond poffiblitie of pee-cing ; yet this one inequality of right on Sir *Philip's* fide, made the propounder calm ; and by coming to terms of expoftulation, did not only reconcile thofe two worthy fpirits , one to another, more firmly than before ; but withall through himfelf wrought, if not a kind of unitie between the Earl of *Leicefter*, and the Count *Hollock* , at leaft a finall fur-ceafe of all violent jealoufies or facti-ous expoftulations.

Thefe particulars I only point out, leaving the reft for them, that may,

per-

perchance, write larger ftories of that
time. To be fhort ; not in complements and art, but reall proofe given
of his fufficience above oth ers ,in very little time his reputation, and authority amongft that active people
grew fo faft, as it had been no hard
matter for him, with the difadvantage of his Uncle, and diftraction of
our affairs in thofe parts, to have raifed himfelf a fortune there. But in
the whole courfe of his life, he did fo
conftantly ballance ambition with
the fafe precepts of divine, and moral duty, as no pretence whatfoever
could have entifed that Gentleman,
to break through the circle of a good
Patriot.

❖❖❖❖❖❖❖❖❖❖❖❖❖❖❖❖❖❖❖❖❖❖

## CHAP. XII

THus fhall it fuffice me to have
trod out fome fteps of this *Bri-
tane Scipio*, thereby to give the learned a fcantling, for drawing out the
L                      reft

reſt of his dimenſions by proportion. And to the end the abruptneſs of this Treatiſe may ſuit more equally with his fortune, I will cut off his Actions, as God did his Life, in the midſt; and ſo conclude with his death.

In which paſſage, though the pride of fleſh, and glory of Mankind be commonly ſo allyed, as the beholders ſeldome ſee any thing elſe in it, but objects of horror, and pittie; yet had the fall of this man ſuch natural degrees, that the wound whereof he died, made rather an addition, than diminution to his ſpirits. So that he ſhewed the world, in a ſhort progreſs to a long home, paſſing fair, and weldrawn lines ; by the guide of which, all pilgrims of this life may conduct themſelves humbly into the haven of everlaſting reſt.

When that unfortunate ſtand was to be made before *Zutphen*, to ſtop the iſſuing out of the Spaniſh Army from a ſtreict ; with what alacrity ſoever

ever

ever he went to actions of honor, yet remembring that upon juft grounds the ancient Sages defcribe the worthieft perfons to be ever beft armed, he had compleatly put on his; but meeting the Marfhall of the Camp lightly armed (whofe honour in that art would not fuffer this unenvious *Themiftocles* to fleep) the unfpotted emulation of his heart, to venture without any inequalitie, made him caft off his Cuiffes; and fo, by the fecret influence of deftinie, to difarm that part, where God (it feems) had refolved to ftrike him. Thus they go on, every man in the head of his own Troop; and the weather being mifty, fell unawares upon the enemie, who had made a ftrong ftand to receive them, near to the very walls of *Zutphen*; by reafon of which accident their Troops fell, not only unexpectedly to be engaged within the levell of the great fhot, that played from the Rampiers, but more fatally with-

in

in fhot of their Mufkets, which were layd in ambufh within their own trenches.

Now whether this were a defperate cure in our Leaders, for a defperate difeafe ; or whether mifprifion, neglect, audacity, or what elfe induced it, it is no part of my office to determine, but onely to make the narration clear, and deliver rumor, as it paffed then, without any ftain, or enammel.

Howfoever, by this ftand, an unfortunate hand out of thofe forefpoken Trenches, brake the bone of Sir *Philip's* thigh with a Mufket-fhot. The horfe he rode upon, was rather furioufly cholleric, than bravely proud , and fo forced him to forfake the field, but not his back, as the nobleft and fitteft biere to carry a Martiall Commander to his grave. In which fad progrefs, paffing along by the reft of the Army, where his Uncle the Generall was, and being
thirftie

thirftie with excefs of bleeding , he
called for drink, which was prefently brought him ; but as he was putting the bottle to his mouth, he faw
a poor Souldier carryed along, who
had eaten his laft at the fame Feaft,
gaftly cafting up his eyes at the
bottle. Which Sir *Philip* perceiving, took it from his head, before
he drank , and delivered it to the
poor man, with thefe words , *Thy*
*necefsity is yet greater than mine.*
And when he had pledged this poor
fouldier, he was prefently carried to
*Arnheim.*

Where the principal Chirurgions
of the Camp attended for him; fome
mercinarily out of gain, others out
of honour to their Art, but the moft
of them with a true zeal (compoun-
ded of love and reverence ) to doe
him good , and ( as they thought )
many Nations in him. When they
began to drefs his wound, he both
by way of charge, and advice, told
them

them, that while his ftrength was
yet entire, his body free from feaver,
and his mind able to endure, they
might freely ufe their art, cut, and
fearch to the bottome. For befides
his hope of health, he would make
this farther profit of the pains
which he muft fuffer, that they
fhould bear witnefs, they had indeed
a fenfible natured man under their
hands, yet one to whom a ftronger
Spirit had given power above himfelf, either to do, or fuffer. But if
they fhould now negleƈt their Art,
and renew torments in the declination of nature, their ignorance, or
over-tendernefs would prove a kind
of tyranny to their friend, and confequently a blemifh to their reverend
fcience.

With love and care well mixt,
they began the cure, and continued
it fome fixteen dayes, not with hope,
but rather fuch confidence of his
recovery, as the joy of their
　　　　　　　　　　　　　　hearts

hearts over-flowed their difcretion, and made them fpread the intelligence of it to the *Queen*, and all his noble friends here in *England*, where it was received, not as private, but publique good news.

Onely there was one Owle among all the birds, which though looking with no lefs zealous eyes than the reft, yet faw, and prefaged more defpair: I mean an excellent Chirurgion of the Count *Hollocks*, who although the Count himfelf lay at the fame inftant hurt in the throat with a Mufket fhot, yet did he neglect his own extremitie to fave his friend, and to that end had fent him to Sir *Philip*. This Chirurgion notwithftanding (out of love to his Mafter) returning one day to drefs his wound, the Count cheerfully afked him how Sir *Philip* did? And being anfwered with a heavy countenance, that he was not well; at thefe words the worthy Prince ( as having more

fenfe

fenfe of his friends wounds, than his own) cries out, Away villain, never fee my face again, till thou bring better news of that mans recovery; for whofe redemption many fuch as I were happily loft.

This honourable act I relate, to give the world one modern example; firft, that greatnefs of heart is not dead every where; and then, that war is both a fitter mould to fafhion it, and ftage to act it on, than peace can be; and laftly, that the reconciliation of enemies may prove fafe, and honourable, where the ciment on either fide is worth. So as this *Florentine* precept concerning reconciled enemies, deferves worthily to be buried with unworthines the author of it, or at leaft the practife of it cryed down, and banifhed, to reign among barbarous heathen fpirits, who while they think life the uttermoft of all things, hold it fafe in no body that their own errors make
doubt-

doubtfull to them. And fuch feems every man that moves any paffion, but pleafure, in thofe intricate natures.

Now after the fixteenth day was paft, and the very fhoulder-bones of this delicate Patient worn through his skin, with conftant, and obedient pofturing of his body to their Art; he judicioufly obferving the pangs his wound ftang him with by fits, together, with many other fymptoms of decay, few or none of recovery, began rather to fubmit his body to thefe Artifts, than any farther to believe in them. Duringwhich fufpenfe, he one morning lifting up the clothes for change & eafe of his body, fmelt fome extraordinary noifom favor about him, differing from oyls and falvs, as he conceived; & either out of naturall delicacy, or at leaft care not to offend others, grew a little troubled with it; which they that fate by perceiving, befought him to let them know

know what fuddain indifpofition he
felt? Sir *Philip* ingenuoufly told it, and
defired them as ingenuoufly to confefs, whether they felt any fuch noi-
fome thing, or no? They all protefted
againft it upon their credits. Whence
Sir *Philip* prefently gave this fevere
doom upon himfelf, that it was inward mortification, and a welcome
meffenger of death

Shortly after, when the Chirurgions
came to drfs him, he acquainted
them with thefe piercing intelligen-
ces between him, and his mortality.
Which though they opened by authority of books, paralleling of acci-
dents, and other artificiall probabilities; yet moved they no alteration in
this man, who judged too truly of his
own eftate, and from more certain
grounds, than the vanity of opinion
in erring artificers could poffibly
pierce into So that afterwards, how
freely foever he left his body fubject
to their practife, and continued a patient

tient beyond exception ; yet did he
not change his minde; but as having
caſt off all hope, or deſire of recove-
rie , made , and divided that little
ſpan of life which was left him in
this manner.

❧✣❧✣❧✣✣❧✣❧✣❧✣❧✣❧✣❧✣❧✣❧✣❧✣

## CHAP. XIII.

FIrſt, he called the Miniſters unto
him ; who were all excellent
men, of divers Nations, and before
them made ſuch a confeſſion of Chriſtian faith , as no book but the heart
can truly, and feelingly deliver. Then
deſired them to accompany him in
Prayer, wherein hee beſought leave
to lead the aſſembly, in reſpect, ( as
he ſaid)that the ſecret ſins of his own
heart were beſt known to himſelf
and out of that true ſenſe , he more
properly inſtructed to apply the e-
ternall

ternall Sacrifice of our Saviours Paffion and Merits to him. His religious Zeal prevailed with this humbly devout, & afflicted company; In which wel chofen progrefs of his, howfoever they were all moved, and thofe fweet motions witneffed by fighes and tears, even interrupting their common devotion; yet could no man judge in himfelf, much lefs in others, whether this rake of heavenly agony, whereupon they all ftood, were forced by forrow for him, or admiration of him; the fire of this *Phenix* hardly being able out of any afhes to produce his equall, as they conceived.

Here this firft mover ftayed the motions in every man, by ftaying himfelf. Whether to give reft to that frail wounded flefh of his, unable to bear the bent of eternity fo much affected, any longer; or whether to abftract that fpirit more inwardly, and by chewing as it were the cudd of medi-

meditation, to imprint thofe excellent images in hs foul ; who can
judge but God ? Notwithftanding,
in this change, (it fhould feem)there
was little,or no change in the objeƈt.
For inftantly after prayer, he entrea-
ted this quire of divine Philofophers
about him, to deliver the opinion of
the ancient Heathen, touching the
immortality of the foul : Firft,to fee
what true knowledge fhe retains of
her own effence, out of the light of
her felf; then to parallel with it the
moft pregnant authorities of the old,
and new Teftament, as fupernatural
revelations,fealed up from our flefh,
for the divine light of faith to re-
veal, and work by. Not that he wanted inftruƈtion or affurance ; but becaufe this fixing of a lovers thoughts
upon thofe externall beauties, was
not only a cheering up of his decay-
ing fpirits, but as it were a taking
poffeffion of that immortall inheritance, which was given unto him by
his

his brother-hood in CHRIST.

The next change uſed, was the calling for his Will ; which though at firſt ſight it may ſeem a deſcent from heaven to earth again; yet he that obſerves the diſtinction of thoſe offices, which he practiſed in beſtowing his own, ſhall diſcern, that as the ſoul of man is all in all, and all in every part ; ſo was the goodnes of his nature equally diſperſed, into the greateſt, and leaſt actions of his too ſhort life. Which Will of his, will ever remain for a witneſs to the world, that thoſe ſweet, and large, even dying affections in him, could no more be contracted with the narrownes of pain, grief, or ſicknes, than any ſparkle of our immortality can bee privately buried in the ſhadow of death.

Here again this reſtlefs ſoul of his (changing only the aire, and not the cords of her harmony ) cals for Muſick; eſpecially that ſong which him-
                                    ſelf

felf had intitled , *La cuiſſe rompue*.
Partly ( as I conceive by the name)
to ſhew that the glory of mortal fleſh
was ſhaken in him : and by that Muſick it ſelf, to faſhion and enfranchiſe
his heavenly ſoul into that everlaſting harmony of Angels, whereof
theſe Concords were a kinde of ter-
reſtriall *Echo* :. And in this ſupreme,
or middle Orb of Contemplations,
he bleſſedly went on , within a
circular motion, to the end of all
fleſh.

The laſt ſcene of this Tragedy
was the parting between the two
brothers : the weaker ſhewing infinite ſtrength in ſuppreſſing ſorrow,
and the ſtronger infinite weakneſs
in expreſſing of it. So far did invaluable worthineſſe, in the dying brother enforce the living to deſcend
beneath his owne worth, and by a-
bundance of childiſh tears, bewail
the publique, in his particular loſs.
Yea ſo far was his true remiſſion
of

of minde transformed into ejulati-
on, that Sir *Philip*, ( in whom all
earthly paſſion did even as it were
flaſh, like lights ready to burn out )
recals thoſe ſpirits together with a
ſtrong vertue, but weak voice;mild-
ly blaming him for relaxing the frail
ſtrengths left to ſupport him, in his
finall combate of ſeparation at hand.
And to ſtop this naturall torrent of
affeſtion in both, took his leave,
with theſe admoniſhing words :

*Love my Memorie , cheriſh my*
*Friends ; their Faith to me may*
*aſſure you they are honeſt. But*
*above all , govern your Will ,*
*and Affeſtions , by the Will and*
*Word of your Creator ; in me,*
*beholding the end of this World,*
*with all her Vanities.*

And

And with this Fare-well, defired the company to lead him away. Here this noble Gentleman ended, the too fhort Scene his life; in which path, whofoever is not confident that he walked the next way to eternall reft, will be found to judge uncharitably.

Thus you fee how it pleafed God to fhew forth, and then fuddenly withdraw this precious light of our skie; and in fome fort adopted Patriot of the States Generall. Between whom, and him, there was fuch a fympathie of affe&tions ; as they honoured that exorbitant worth in *Sir Philip*, by which time, and occafion had been like enough to metamorphofe this new Ariftocracy of theirs into their ancient, and much honoured forme of *Dukedome*. And he again applauded that univerfall ingenuitie, and profperous undertakings of theirs ; over which perchance he felt fomething in his own nature, poffible in time to come an ele&t Commander. So ufuall is it for all mortall conftitu-

M                    tions,

tions, to affect that, which infenfibly often works change in them to better, or worfe.

Now though I am not of their faith, who affirme wife men can governe the Starres;yet do I beleeve no Star-gazers can fo well prognofticate the good, or ill of all Governments, as the providence of men trained up in publique affaires may doe. Whereby they differ from Prophets only in this ; that Prophets by infpiration, and thefe by confequence, judge of things to come.

Amongft which kind of Prophets, give me leave to reckon this Gentleman; who firft having, out of the credible *Almanach* of Hiftory, regiftred the growth, health, difeafe, and periods of Governments : that is to fay,when Monarchies grow ready for change , by over-relaxing, or contracting, when the ftates of few, or many continue, or forfake to be the fame : and in the conftant courfe of thefe viciffitudes,having forefeen the eafie fatietie of mankinde with

Re-

Religion, and Government, their naturall difccntentment with the prefent,
and aptneffe to welcome alteration :
And againe, in the defcent of each particular forme to her owne centre, having obferved how thefe United Provinces had already changed from their
ancient Dukedomes to Popularitie :
and yet in that Popularitie, been forced
to feek protection among the Monarchies then raigning ; and to make perfect this judgment of his, had fumm'd
up the league offenfive, and defenfive
between us, and them ; even then he
grew doubtfull, left this advantage
would in time leave latitude for envy,
and competencie, to work fome kind of
rent in our Union.

But when in the progreffe of this
profpect, he fell into a more particular
confideration of their traffique, and
ours : they without any native commodities (Art and diligence excepted) making themfelves Mafters of wealth in
all Nations : We againe, by exporting
our

our substantiall riches, to import a superfluous masse of trifles, to the vaine exhausting of our home-borne staple commodities; he certainly concluded, that this true Philosophers stone of traffique, which not only turned base mettals into gold, but made profit by Wars in their owne bosomes, would infallibly stir up emulation in such lookers on, as were far from striving otherwise to imitate them.

And out of these or the like grounds hath many times told me, that this active people (which held themselves constantly to their Religion, and Freedome)would at length grow from an adjective to a substantive, and prosperous subsistence. Whereas we on the other side, dividing our selves, and waving in both, should first become jealous, then strange to our friends, and in the end (by reconciliation with our common enemie) moderate that zeale, wherein excesse only is the meane; and so be forced to cast our fortunes into their armes

armes for fupport, who are moſt inte-
reſted in our diſhonour, and ruine.
Theſe with many other dangers (which
he proviſionally feared) howſoever the
wiſdome of our Government may perchance have put off by prevention : yet
were more then conjecturall in the
afpect of fuperior, inferior, forraigne,
and domeſtique Princes then raigning.

But fuppofe we could not by this
Kalender comprehend the change of
Afpects, and Policies in feverall Kingdomes ; yet we may at leaſt therein diſ-
cerne, both the judgment of this *Prome-
theus* concerning our felves, and the tender affection he carried to that oppreffed Nation. Which refpect of his they
againe fo well underſtood, as after his
death the States of *Zealand* became fui-
tors to her Majeſty, & his noble friends,
that they might have the honour of bu-
rying his body at the publique expence
of their Government. A memorable
wiſdome of thankfulneſſe, by well
handling the dead, to encourage, and
mul-

multiply faith in the living.

Which requeſt had it been granted, the Reader may pleaſe to conſider, what Trophies it is likely they would have erected over him, for poſterity to admire, and what inſcriptions would have been deviſed for eternizing his memory. Indeed fitter for a great, and brave Nation to enlarge, then the capacitie, or good will of a private, and inferior friend. For my own part I confeſſe, in all I have here ſet downe of his worth, and goodneſſe; I find my ſelf ſtill ſhort of that honour he deſerved, and I deſired to doe him.

I muſt therefore content my ſelfe with this poor demonſtration of homage; and ſo proceed to ſay ſomewhat of the toyes, or Pamphlets, which I inſcribe to his memory, as monuments of true affection between us; whereof (you ſee) death hath no power.

*CAP.*

## CAP. XIV.

WHen my youth, with favour of Court in fome moderate proportion to my birth, and breeding in the activeneffe of that time, gave mee opportunity of moft bufineffe : then did my yet undifcouraged Genius moft affect to finde, or make work for it felf. And out of that freedom, having many times offered my fortune to the courfe of Forraigne employments, as the proprieft forges to fafhion a Subject for the reall fervices of his Soveraigne ; I found the returnes of thofe mif-placed endeavours to prove, both a vaine charge to my felfe, and an offenfive undertaking to that excellent Governeffe, over all her Subjects duties and affections.

For inftance, how mild foever thofe mixtures of favours, and corrections

M 4 were

were in that Princely Lady : yet to
shew that they fell heavy in crossing a
young mans ends ; I will onely choose,
and alleage foure out of many, some
with leave, some without.

First, when those two mighty Armies of *Don Iohns*, and the Duke *Cafimires*, were to meet in the Low
Countries ; my Horses, with all
other preparations being shipped at
*Dover*, with leave under her Bill assigned : Even then was I stayed by a
Princely Mandate, the Messenger Sir
*Edward Dier*. Wherein whatsoever
I felt, yet I appeale to the judicious
Reader, whether there be any latitude
left (more then humble obedience) in
these nice cases between duty, and selfenesse, in a Soveraignes service ?

After this, when Mr Secretary *Walfingham* was sent Embassador, to treate
with those two Princes in a businesse
so much concerning Christian blood,
and Christian Empires ; then did the
same irregular motion (which seldome
rests,

refts, but fleales where it cannot trade) perfwade me, that whofoever would venture to go without leave, was fure never to bee ftayed. Upon which falfe axiome (trufting the reft to chance) I went over with Mr Secretary, unknown: But at my returne was forbidden her prefence for many moneths.

Againe, when my Lord of *Leicefter* was fent Generall of Her Majefties Forces into the *Low Countries*, and had given me the command of an hundred Horfe; then I giving my humors over to good order, yet found, that neither the earneft interceffion of this Grandee, feconded with mine own humble fute, and many other Honourable Friends of mine, could prevaile againft the conftant courfe of this excellent Lady with her Servants. So as I was forced to tarry behind; and for this importunity of mine to change my courfe, and feem to preferre nothing before my fervice about her : This

Princeffe

Princefle of Government, as well as Kingdomes, made me live in her Court a fpectacle of dif-favour, too long as I conceived.

Laftly, the univerfall fame of a battle to bee fought, between the prime Forces of *Henry* the third, and the religious of *Henry* the fourth, then King of *Navarre*; lifting me yet once more above this humble earth of duty, made me refolve to fee the difference between Kings prefent, and abfent in their Martiall Expeditions. So that without acquainting any creature, the Earle of *Effex* excepted, I fhipped my felfe over : and at my returne, was kept from her prefence full fix moneths, and then received after a ftrange manner. For this abfolute Prince, to fever ill example from grace, averrs my going over to bee a fecret imployment of Hers : and all thefe other petty exiles, a making good of that cloud, or figure, which fhe was pleafed to caft over my abfence. Protecting me to the world

with

with the honour of her imployment,
rather then fhe would, for examples
fake, be forced either to punifh mee
farther, or too eafily forgive a contempt, or negle&, in a Servant fo near
about her, as fhe was pleafed to conceive it.

By which many warnings, I finding
the fpecious fires of youth to prove far
more fcorching, then glorious, called
my fecond thoughts to counfell, and in
that Map cleerly difcerning A&ion,
and Honor, to fly with more wings
then one : and that it was fufficient
for the plant to grow where his Sove-
raignes hand had planted it; I found
reafon to contra& my thoughts from
thofe larger, but wandring *Horizons,*
of the world abroad, and bound my
profpe& within the fafe limits of duty,
in fuch home fervices, as were accepta-
ble to my Soveraigne.

In which retired view, Sir *Philip
Sidney,* that exa& image of quiet, and
a&ion : happily united in him, and
feldome

feldome well divided in any; being
ever in mine eyes, made me thinke it
no fmall degree of honour to imitate,
or tread in the fteps of fuch a Leader.
So that to faile by his Compaffe, was
fhortly (as I faid) one of the principall
reafons I can alleage, which perfwaded
me to fteale minutes of time from my
daily fervices, and employ them in this
kind of writing.

Since my declining age, it is true,
that I had (for fome yeeres) more leafure to difcover their imperfections,
then care, or induftry to amend them:
finding in my felfe, what all men com-
plaine of in the world, that it is more
eafie to finde fault, excufe, or tolerate,
then to examine and reforme.

The workes (as you fee) are Tragedies, with fome Treatifes annexed. The
Treatifes (to fpeake truly of them)
were firft intended to be for every Act
a Chorus: and though not borne out of
the prefent matter acted, yet being the
largeft fubjects I could then think upon,

on, and no fuch ftrangers to the fcope
of the Tragedies, but that a favourable
Reader might eafily find fome confan-
guinitie between them;I preferring this
generall fcope of profit, before the felf-
reputation of being an exaƈt Artifan in
that Poeticall Myftery, conceived that
a perfpeƈtive into vice, and the unprof-
perities of it,would prove more accep-
table to every good Readers ends, then
any bare murmur of difcontented fpirits againft their prefent Government,
or horrible periods of exorbitant paffions among equals.

Which with humble fayles after I
had once ventured upon this fpreading
*Ocean* of Images, my apprehenfive
youth, for lack of a well touched compaffe, did eafily wander beyond proportion. And in my old age againe, looking
back on them with a fathers eye:when I
confidered firft, how poorly the inward
natures of thofe glorious names were
expreffed :then how much eafier it was
to excufe deformities, then to cure
them;

them ; though I found reason to change their places, yet I could not find in my heart to bestow cost, or care, in altering their light, and limited apparell in verse.

From hence to come particularly to that Treatise intitled: *The Declination of Monarchy*. Let me beg leave of the favourable Reader, to bestow a few lines more in the story of this Changling, then I have done in the rest ; and yet to use no more serious authority then the rule of *Diogenes*, which was, to hang the Posie where there is most need.

The first birth of that *Phantasme* was divided into three parts, with intention of the Author, to be disposed amongst their fellows, into three diverse Acts of the Tragedies. But (as I said before) when upon a second review, they, and the rest were all ordain'd to change their places; then did I (like an old, and fond Parent, unlike to get any more children) take pains rather to cover the dandled deformities of these creatures

with

with a coat of many feames, then care-
lefly to drive them away, as birds doe
their young ones.

Yet againe, when I had in mine own
cafe well weigh'd the renderneffe of
that great fubject and confequently, the
nice path I was to walke in between two
extremities; but efpecially the danger,
by treading afide, to caft fcandall upon
the facred foundations of Monarchy;
together with the fate of many Meta-
phyficall *Phormio's* before me, who had
loft themfelves in teaching Kings, and
Princes, how to governe their People:
then did this new profpect dazzle mine
eyes, and fufpend my travell for a time.

But the familiar felf-love, which is
more or leffe born in every man, to live,
and dye with him, prefently moved me
to take this Bear-whelp up againe and
licke it. Wherein I, rowfing my felfe
under the banner of this flattery, went
about (as a fond mother) to put on rich-
er garments, in hope to adorne them.
But while thefe clothes were in making,

I

I perceived that coſt would but draw more curious eyes to obſerve deformities. So that from theſe checks a new counſell roſe up in me, to take away all opinion of ſeriouſneſſe from theſe perplexed pedegrees; and to this end careleſly caſt them into that hypocriticall figure *Ironia*, wherein men commonly (to keep above their workes) ſeeme to make toies of the utmoſt they can doe.

And yet againe, in that confuſing miſt, when I beheld this grave ſubject (which ſhould draw reverence and attention) to bee over ſpangled with lightneſſe, I forced in examples of the Roman gravity, and greatneſſe, the harſh ſeverity of the *Lacedemonian* Government; the riches of the *Athenian* learning, wit, and induſtry; and like a man that plaies divers parts upon ſeverall hints, left all the indigeſted crudities, equally applied to Kings, or Tyrants : whereas in every cleere judgement, the right line had beene

                                    ſufficient

sufficient enough to difcover the crooked ; if the image of it could have proved credible to men.

Now for the feverall branches, or difcourfes following ; they are all Members of one, and the fame imperfect body, fo as I let them take their fortunes (like Effayes) onely to tempt, and ftir up fome more free Genius, to fafhion the whole frame into finer mould for the worlds ufe. The firft limme of thofe Treaties (I mean that Fabrick of a fuperftitious Church) having by her mafterfull ambition over Emperours, Kings, Princes, free States, and Councels, with her *Conclave* deceits, ftrengths, and unthankfulneffe, fpred fo far beyond my *Horizon*, as I at once gave over her, and all her derivations to *Gamaliels* infallible cenfure; Leaving Lawes, Nobility, War, Peace, and the reft, (as glorious Trophies of our old Pope, the fin) to change, reforme, or become deformed, according as vanity, that limit-

N                          leffe

litle mother of thefe Idolatries, fhould either winne of the truth, or the truth of them.

Laftly, concerning the Tragedies themfelves; they were in their firft creation three; Whereof *Antonie* and *Cleopatra*, according to their irregular paffions, in forfaking Empire to follow fenfuality, were facrificed to the fire. The executioner, the author himfelfe. Not that he conceived it to be a contemptible younger brother to the reft : but left while he feemed to looke over much upward, hee might ftumble into the Aftronomers pit. Many members in that creature (by the opinion of thofe few eyes, which faw it) having fome childifh wantonneffe in them, apt enough to be conftrued, or ftrained to a perfonating of vices in the prefent Governors, and government.

From which cautious profpect, I bringing into my minde the ancient Poets, metamorphofing mans reafonable

ble nature into the fenfitive of beafts,
or vegetative of plants ; and knowing
thefe all (in their true morall) to bee
but images of the unequall ballance
between humors, and times ; nature,
and place. And again in the practice
of the world, feeing the like inftance
not poetically, but really fafhioned in
the Earle of *Effex* then falling; and
ever till then worthily beloved both of
*Queen*, and people · This fudden defcent of fuch greatneffe, together with
the quality of the Actors in every
Scene, ftir'd up the Authors fecond
thoughts, to bee carefull (in his owne
cafe) of leaving faire weather behind
him. Hee having, in the Earles precipitate fortune, curioufly obferved :
Firft, how long this Noblemans birth,
worth, and favour had been flattered,
tempted, and ftung by a fwarm of Sect-
animals, whofe property was to wound,
and fly away : and fo, by a continuall
affliction probably enforce great hearts
to turne, and toffe for eafe ; and in

thofe

thofe paffive poftures, perchance to tumble fometimes upon their Sove-raignes Circles.

Into which pitfall of theirs, when they had once difcerned this Earle to be fallen; ftraight, under the reverend ftile of *Lafa Majeftas*, all inferiour Minifters of Juftice (they knew) would be juftly let loofe to work upon him. And accordingly, under the fame cloud, his enemies took audacity to caft Libels abroad in his name a-gainft the State, made by themfelves; fet papers npon pofts, to bring his innocent friends in queftion. His power, by the Jefuiticall craft of ru-mor, they made infinite; and his am-bition more then equall to it. His Letters to private men were read o-penly, by the the piercing eyes of an Atturnies Office, which warranteth the conftruction of every time in the worft fenfe againft the writer.

My felfe, his Kinfman, and while I remained about the *Queen*, a kinde of
*Remora*,

*Remora,* ſtaying the violent courſe of that fatall Ship, and theſe winde-watching Paſſengers(at leaſt,as his ene-mies imagined) abruptly ſent away to guard a figurative Fleet, in danger of nothing, but theſe *Proſopopeia's* of invi-ſible rancor; and kept (as in a free Priſon) at *Rocheſter,* till his head was off.

Before which ſudden journey, ca-ſting mine eyes upon the catching Court ayres, which I was to part from; I diſcerned my Gracious Soveraigne to bee every way ſo invironed with theſe, not *Iupiters,* but *Pluto's* thunder-workers; as it was impoſſible for Her to ſee any light, that might lead to grace, or mercy : but many encoura-ging Meteors of ſeverity, as againſt an unthankfull favourite, and traiterous Subject ; hee ſtanding, by the Law of *England,* condemned for ſuch.

So that let his heart bee (as in my conſcience it was) free from this unna-turall crime, yet theſe *unreturning*

N 3            ſteps

steps feemed well worth the obferving. Efpecially in the cafe of fuch a Favorite, as never put his Soveraigne to ftand between her People, and his errors ; but here, and abroad placed his body in the forefront, againft all that either threatned, or affaulted Her.

And being no Admirall, nor yet a Creator of Admiralls, whereby feare, or hope might have kept thofe temporary *Neptunes* in a kinde of fubjection to him ; yet hee freely ventured himfelfe in all Sea-actions of his time. As if he would war the greatneffe of envy, place, and power, with the greatneffe of worth, and incomparable induftry. Neverthelelffe hee wanted not judgement to difcerne, that whether they went with him, or tarried behind, they muft probably prove unequall yoke fellowes in the one; or *in* the other paffing curious, and carping judges over all his publike Actions.

Againe, this gallant young Earle, created (as it feemes) for action, before

fore he was Martiall, firſt as a privace
Gentleman, and after as a Lieutenant
by Commiſſion, went in the head of
all our Land Troops, that marched in
his time ; and beſides experience, ſtill
wan ground, even through competen-
cy, envy, and confuſed mixtures of
equality or inequality, amongſt the
factious Engliſh, all inferiour in his
owne active worth, and merit.

Laſtly, he was ſo far from affecting
the abſolute power of *Henry* the thirds
Favourites, I meane under a King to
become equall at leaſt with him, in creating and depoſing Chancellors, Treaſurers, and Secretaries of State, to
raiſe a ſtrong party for himſelfe ; as
he left both place, and perſons entire in
their ſupreme juriſdictions, or Ma-
giſtracies under his Soveraigne, as ſhee
granted them. And though hee foreſaw a neceſſary diminution of their
peacefull predicaments by his carrying
up the ſtandard of *Mars* ſo high, and
withall knew they (like wiſe men) muſt

N 4　　　　　　　as

as cerrainly difcern, that the rifing of
his, or falling of their fcales depended
upon the profperity, or unprofperity
of his undertakings : yet (I fay) that
active heart of his freely chofe to hazard himfelfe upon their cenfures,
without any other provifionall ram-
pier againft the envious, and fuppref-
fing crafts of that party, then his owne
hope, and refolution to deferve well.

Neither did he (like the French Favorites of that time) ferve his own humors or neceffities, by felling feats of
Juftice, Nobility, or orders of honor,
till they became *Colliers pour toute befte*,
to the difparagement of creating power, and difcouraging of the Subjects
hope, or induftry, in attaining to advancement, or profit : But fuffered
*England* to ftand alone, in her ancient
degrees of freedomes, and integrities,
and fo referved that abfolute power of
Creation facred in his Soveraigne,
without any mercenary ftaine, or allay.

CAP.

## *CAP. XV.*

NOw after this humble, and harm-
leffe defire of a meane fubject, expreffed in qualifying a great fubjects
errors, by the circumftance of fuch inftruments, as naturally (like Bats) both
flye, and prey in the darke; Let the Reader pardon me, if I prefume yet againe
to multiply digreffion upon digreffion,
in honour of her, to whom I owe my
felfe, I meane *Queen Elizabeth :* and in
her name clearly to know, that though
I lament the fall of this great man in
Ifrael, nevertheleffe the truth enforceth
me to confeffe, that howfoever thefe
kinds of high juftice may fometimes
(like the uttermoft of the Law) fall
heavy upon one brave fpirit; yet prove
they mercy to many by example : and
therefore as Regall, and Royall wifedomes, ought to be honoured equally
*in*

in all the differing Soveraignties
through the world, of one, few or many.

And if this *aſſumpſit* muſt be granted univerſally ; then how much more
in the caſe of ſuch a Princeſſe, as (even
while ſhe was ſubjeȼt) left patternes
that might inſtruȼt all ſubjeȼts, rather
to undergoe the indignation of Sove-
raignes with the birthright of duty,
then with the mutiny of over ſenſible,
and rebellious affeȼtions ; which ever
(like diſeaſed pulſes)beat faſter,or ſlow-
er then they ſhould, to ſhew all to be
infeȼted about them ? Whereas this
Lady,in the like ſtraines,by an humble,
and conſtant temper, had already with
true obedience triumphed over the curious examinations of aſcending flattery, or deſcending Tyranny, even in
the tenderneſſe of Princes ſucceſſions.

And to make this manifeſt to bee
choice, and not chance : even when her
ſtepmother misfortune grew ripe for
delivery,then was ſhe neither born cry-
ing,

ing, as children be : nor yet by the fudden change from a prifon, to a Throne, came fhe upon that Stage confufedly barking after all that had offended : but like one borne to behold true light, inftantly fixeth her thoughts upon larger notions then revenge, or favour. And in the infancy of her Raigne, cals for *Benefield* her hard-hearted Gaoler ; bids him enjoy not a deferved, but free given peace under his narrow vine : with this affurance, that whenfoever fhe defired to have prifoners over feverely intreated, fhe would not forget to commit the cuftody of them to his charge.

Againe, for the next object, looking backward upon her fifters Raigne, fhe obferves Religion to have been changed; Perfecution, like an ill weed, fuddenly grown up to the higheft ; The mercy of the infinite perfcribed, by abridgment of time, and adding torments to the death of his creatures : falvation publifhed in many more *Creeds* then fhe was taught to beleeve: A double Supremacy

in

in one Kingdome; *Rome* become Empe-
rour of the Clergy, and by bewitching
the better halfe of man (I meane the
foule) challenging both over Clergy,
and Laity, the ftile of the *Great God :*
*Rex Regum, Dominus Dominantium.*

This view brought forth in her a
vow, like that of the holy Kings in the
Old Teftament; *viz.*that fhe would neither hope, nor feeke for reft in the mortall traffique of this world, till fhe had
repaired the precipitate ruines of our
*Saviours Militant Church*, through all
her Dominions ; and as fhe hoped, in
the reft of the World, by her example.
Upon which Princelike refolution, this
She-*David* of ours ventured to undertake the great *Goliath* among the *Phili-*
*ftins* abroad, I mean *Spain* and the *Pope* ;
defpifeth their multitudes, not of men,
but of Hofts ; fcornfully rejecteth that
Holy Fathers wind-blowne fuperftitions, and takes the (almoft folitary)
truth for her Leading-Star.

Yet tears fhe not the Lyons jawes in
funder

funder at once, but moderately begins
with her own Changlings ; gives the
Bishops a proper motion,but bounded:
the Nobility time to reforme themfelves,with inward,and outward Councell ; revives her Brothers Lawes for
eftablifhing of the Churches doctrine,
and difcipline, but moderates their
feverity of proceeding ; gives frailty,
and fect, time to reforme at home : and
in the mean feafon fupplyes the Prince
of *Conde* with men,and money, as chief
among the Proteftants in *France* ; gathers, and revives the fcattered hofts of
Ifrael at the worft : takes *New-Haven*,
perchance with hope of redeeming *Callice*, to the end her axle-trees might
once againe lie upon both fhores,as her
right did : refufeth marriage,reformes
and redeemes Queen *Maries* vanities,
who firft glorying in the Spanifh feed,
publifheth that fhe was with childe,
and inftantly offers up that Royall fuppofed Iffue of hers, together with the
abfolute Government of all her Natives

tives to the mixt Tyranny of *Rome* and *Castile.*

In which endlesse path of servitude, the Noune adjective nature of this superstitious Princesse, proceeded yet a degree further ; striving to confirme that double bondage of people, and Posterity, by Act of Parliament. Where on the other side, the Spanish King, beholding these remisse homages of frailty, with the unthankfull, and insatiable eyes of ambition, apprehends these petty sacrifices, as fit strawes, sticks, or feathers, to be pull'd out of faint wings, for the building up, and adorning of a Conquerours nest. And under this Tyrannicall *Crisis*, takes freedome to exhaust her treasure to his owne ends, breakes our league with *France*, and in that breach shakes the sacred foundation of the rest, winnes St *Quintins*, while we lost *Callice.*

Contrary to all which thought-bound Councels of her sister *Maries*, Queen *Elizabeth* (as I said) not yet out of

of danger of her Romiſh ſubjeƈts at
home ; threatned with their mighty
faƈtion,and party abroad ; peſter'd beſides with want of money, and many
binding Lawes of her ſiſters making :
yet like a Palme, under all theſe bur-
dens, ſhe raiſeth her ſelſe Prince-like :
and upon notice of her Agents diſgrace
abroad, his ſervants being put into the
Inquiſition by the Spaniard ; her Merchants ſurprized in *America*, contrary
to the league between *Charles* the fifth,
and *Henry* the eighth ; which gave free
traſſique : *In omnibus,& ſingulis Regnis,
Dominiis, Inſulis*, notwithſtanding that
Aſtronomicall, or rather biaced divi-
ſion of the world by the Popes lines,
which (contrary to the nature of all
lines) only keep latitude for the advantage of *Spain :* She (I ſay) upon theſe
inſolencies, receives the *Hollander*, and
proteƈts him from perſecution of the
Duke of *Alva :* ſettles theſe poore
Refugees in *Norwich, Colcheſter, Sand-
wich, Maidſtone*, and *South-Hampton.*
Yet

Yet againe, when this faith distinguishing Duke appealed to her selfe: she binding her heart for better, or worse, to the words of her Contract; summons these afflicted strangers to depart. Their number was great, their time short, and yet their weather-beaten soules so sensible of long continued oppressions in their liberties, and consciences, as (by the opportunity of this Ostracisme) they in their passage surprized *Brill*, *Flushing*, and diverse other Towns, expulsing the Spaniards; and by this brave example, taught, and proclaimed a way of freedome to all well affected Princes, and Provinces, that were opprest.

Wherein it may please the Reader to observe, that *Henry* the third of *France*, being one in the same League, and belike upon change of heart, which ever brings forth new questions, demanding, whether *mutuall defence against all*, extended to the cause of Religion? was presently answered by her; that she

both

both treated, and concluded in the fame fenfe ; and if it were required at her hands, would performe every branch of it to her uttermoft. The *French King* hereupon makes war with the Proteftants : *Monfieur* his brother fecretly protects them by *Cafimire.*

Againe about that time, at the requeft of the *Spanifh* King, fhe guards his Navy into *Flanders*; where it being loft, and fhe requefted by the fame King to lend him her owne Ships, for recovery of the Maritime Townes fallen from him ; this bleffed *Lady* both denyes this crafty requeft of a Conqueror , and withall providently refufeth any of his fhips to be harboured in her Ports. Yet in honour of her ancient League with the Houfe of *Burgundy*, fhe publifheth the like inhibition to her beloved, and fafe Neighbours the *Netherlands*. And inftantly, with a ftrong judgment in ballancing of forraigne Princes, perfwades the King of *Spain* to make peace with the *Hollanders*, and on the other

Q                           fide

side diswades those distressed *Hollanders* from joyning with *France.* As I conceive, thinking that Kingdome (manumised from us by time) might through the conjunction of the *Holland* shipping, and Mariners, with their disciplin'd Land-Armies of horse and foot, prove more dangerous enemies, either by way of invasion, or incursion( as I said once before) then that Kings glorious Standard, borne among his barbed horse, and light foot had hitherto done, either in our entised undertakings, or abandoned retraits.

Besides it is worthy of reverence in this *Queen,* that she never was afraid, or ashamed to averre the quarrell of Religion for a ground of her friends, or enemies.

And though in the charity of a Christian Prince, even in the danger of a growing faction at home, she was content to let devout conscience live quietly in her Realmes : yet when they began to practise disunion in Church,

as

as their Jefuited fpirits naturally affect
to doe. Then to fhew that fhe was as
well fervant to God, as by him King
over Peoples, fhe tyed the head of
the facrifice perchance a little clofer to
the hornes of the altar. And made thofe
fpirits which would not know the true
God altogether, to have fome kinde of
fenfe, or fmart of his Religious Lawes ;
howfoever they were dead, and facrificed to the growing Supremacy of the
Roman Miter, or conquering Scepter
of *Spaine* ; ordain'd (as fhe thought) by
exceffe of playing faft or loofe with
God, and the world ; in time, one to
devoure the other;ambitious and fuperftitious fubtleties being an Abyffe, or
Sea, where the ftronger infallibly de-
voures the weaker.

  She makes a publique League, for
defence of Religion, with the King of
*Scots, Denmark*, and the Princes of *Germany* ; perfwades a Marriage between
*Scotland* and *Denmark* ; exileth all Je-
fuites, and Seminary Priefts by Act
of

of Parliament; makes it felony to harbor any of them in *England*, or for the English to send any of theirs beyond the Seas, to be trained up among them.

Upon the losse of *Antuerpe*, she resolutely undertakes the protection of the Netherlanders, and to distract the Spaniard (as I said before) sends *Drake* to the *West-Indies*, with 21 Ships, who surprised *Domingo*, and *Cartagena*. And immediately after his returne, with spoile, and triumph (to prevent all possibility of Invasion) she sets him to Sea againe, with Commission to burne all Ships, Gallyes, and Boats, along his Spanish Coasts. Who, in the same Voyage, breaks through diverse of his Gallyes in the Bay of *Cales*, appointed to withstand him; takes, burnes, and drownes 100 Sayle laden with munition, and victuals. From thence in his way to *Capo St Vincent*, he surpriseth three Forts: burnes ships, fisher-boats, and nets; and then making for the *Azores*, hee there takes a Carricke

com-

comming from the *Eaſt-Indies.*

The next yeare (as treading in his
ſteps) *Cavendiſh* returnes from his journey about the world, with the ſpoile of
nineteen Ships, and of many ſmall
Towns in *America.*

This and ſuch like providence did
this miracle of Princes uſe in all her
Wars, whereby her Wars maintained
her wealth, and that wealth ſupplyed
her War. So as ſhe came ever in ſtate,
when ſhe demanded aid from her Houſe
of Commons. Neither did ſhe fetch,
or force preſidents from her Predeceſ-
ſors in thoſe demands:but made her ſelf
a preſident to all Poſterities, that the
love of people to a loving Princeſſe is
not ever curiouſly ballanced, by the
ſelf-pittying abilities of mankinde : but
their ſpirits, hearts, and ſtates being
drawne up above their owne fraile ſelf-
neſſe,the audit is taken after ; and perchance ſumm'd up with a little ſmart to
themſelves, wherein they glory.

Neither did ſhe, by any curious

ſearch

search after Evidence to enlarge her Prerogatives Royall, teach her subjects in Parliament, by the like self-affections, to make as curious inquisition among their Records, to colour any encroaching upon the sacred Circles of Monarchy : but left the rise or fall of these two ballances asleep, with those aspiring spirits, who (by advantage of state, or time taken) had been authors of many biaced motions. And in some confused Parliaments amongst the Barons Wars, even forced her Ancestors, with one breath, to proscribe and restore;to call out of the House of Commons, by Writ, to the upper House, during the Session : Wherein one mans sudden advancement proves envious to foure hundred of his equals ; and from the same, not truly active, but rather passive vaine, to imprison and release unjudicially sometime striving to master the multitude, by their Nobility, then again waving the Nobility with the multitude of people;both marks of disease,

diſeaſe, and no healthfull ſtate in a Monarchy.  All which ſhe providently foreſaw, and avoided; left, by the like inſenſible degrees of miſleading paſſions, ſhe might be conſtrained to deſcend, and labour the compaſſing of diſorderly ends, by a Mechanicall kinde of Univerſity Canvaſſe.

So that this bleſſed, and bleſſing *Lady*, with a calme minde, as well in quiet, as ſtirring times, ſtudied how to keep her ancient under-earth buildings, upon their firſt well laid foundations. And if ſhe found any ſtray'd, rather to reduce them back to their originall circuits, then ſuffer a ſtep to be made over, or beſides thoſe time-authorized aſſemblies.  And by this reſervedneſſe, ever comming upon the ſtage a Commander, and no Petitioner, ſhe preſerv'd her ſtate above the affronts of Nobility, or people; and according to birthright, ſtill became a ſoveraigne Judge over any dutifull, or encroaching petitions of Nobles, or Commons.

O 4            For

For this *Lady*, though not prophetically, yet like a provident Princeſſe, in
the ſeries of things, and times, foreſaw
through the long laſting wiſdome of
Government, a quinteſſence, howſoever
abſtracted out of Morall Philoſophy,
and humane Lawes, yet many degrees
in uſe of mankinde above them. She,
I ſay, foreſaw, that every exceſſe of paſſion expreſt from the Monarch in Acts,
or Councels of Eſtate, would infallibly
ſtir up in the people the like cobwebs
of a popular ſpinning, and therefore
from theſe piercing grounds, ſhe concluded, that a ſteady hand in the government of Soveraignty, would ever prove
more proſperous, then any nimble or
witty practiſe, crafty ſhifting, or Imperious forcing humors poſſibly could
doe.

Againe in the latitudes which ſome
moderne Princes allow to their Favorites, as ſupporters of Government;
and middle wals between power, and
the peoples envy ; it ſeems this *Queen*
re-

refervedly kept entrenched within her native ftrengths, and Scepter.

For even in the height of *Effex* his credit with her, how far was fhe from permitting him (like a *Remus*) to leap over any wall of her new-built Anti-Rome ; or with a young, and unexperienced *genius* to fhuffle Pulpits, Parliaments, Lawes, and other fundamentall eftablifhments of her Kingdomes, into any glorious apparances of will, or power ? It fhould feeme a forefeeing, that howfoever this unexpected racking of people might for a time, in fome particulars, both pleafe, and adde a glofly ftick to enlarge the Eagles neft ; yet that in the end all buildings above the truth, muft neceffarily have forced her two *Supremacies*, of ftate, and nature, to defcend, and through irregularities acted in her name, either become a fanctuary between the world, and inferior perfons errors ; or (as playing an after-game with her fubjects, for a fubject) conftraine her to change the tenure of

comman-

commanding power, into a kind of un-
princely mediation. And for what?
Even vanity to intreat her people, that
they would hope well of diverse confu-
sions: howsoever they might seem hea-
dy, nay ignorant passions: and such as
threaten no lesse, then a losse of native
Liberties, descended upon her people,
by the same prescription of time and
right, by which the Crowne had descended upon her selfe, and her Ancestors; with a probable consequence of
many more sharp pointed Tyrannies
over them and their freedomes, then
their happily deceased Parents ever
tasted or dream't of.

Besides, admit these flatterings, and
threatnings of hope, or feare (which
transcendent power is sometimes forced to worke by) could have drawne
this excellent Princesse, and her time-
present subjects to make brasse an
equally currant standard with gold, or
silver, within her Sea compass'd Dominions; yet abroad, where the freedome
of

of other Soveraignties is bounded by Religion, Juftice, and well-waigh'd commerce amongft Neighbor-Princes, fhe forefaw, the leaft thought of multiplying felf-Prerogatives, there would inftantly be difcredited and refleded back to ftir up difcouragement in the fofteft hearts, of her moft humble and dutifull fubjeds.

Therefore contrary to all thefe captived, and captiving apparances, this experienced Governeffe of ours publifhed to the world, by a conftant *Series* in her adions, that fhe never was, nor ever would be overloaden with any fuch exceffes in her Perfon, or defeds in her Government, as might conftraine her to fupport, or be fupported by a Monopolous ufe of Favourites ; as if fhe would make any greater then her felfe, to governe Tyrannically by them.

Nay more ; fo far off was fhe from any lukewarmneffe in Religion, as if a fingle teftimony may have credit, that bleffed *Queens* many and free difcourfes ses with my selfe, ingeniously bare record; that the unexpected conversion of *Henry* the Fourth fell fatally upon him, by the weaknesses of his Predecessor *Henry* the Third, and the dissolute miscarriage of his Favourites. Who like Lapwings, with the shels of authority about their necks, were let loose to runne over all the branches of his Kingdome, misleading Governors, Nobility, and People from the steady, and mutuall rest of Lawes, Customes, and other ancient wisdomes of government, into the wildernesses of ignorance, and violence of will. Amongst which defects, all fundamentall changes (especially of Religion) in Princes would be found (as she conceived) the true discipline of Atheisme amongst their Subjects; all sacrifices, obedience excepted, being but deare-bought knowledges of the Serpent, to expulse Kings, and People once againe out of Mediocrity, that reciprocall Paradise of mutuall humane duties.

Pro-

Prophetically concluding, that whofoever will fell God to purchafe earth,
by making that eternall unity of many
fhapes, muft in the end make him of
none : and fo bee forced with loffe,
contempt and danger to traffique not
for an heires place, but a younger brothers; in that Church, at whofe wide
gates he had (with fhame enough) already turned in. And under conditions
of a Servant, rather then of a Sonne, be
conftrained for his firft ftep to fet up
the Jefuits faction, providently fuppreffed by himfelfe before, and therein
to fhake the *Sorbonifts*, faithfull fup-
porters in all times of Crowne-Sove-
raignty, againft thefe flave-making
conjunctions betweene the Spaniard,
and his *Chaplaine*. Nay, yet with a
greater fhew of ingratitude, his next
ftep muft be to fuppreffe thofe humble
foules, who had long fupported him,
whileft he was King of *Navarre*, againft
that murthering Holy-water of Spanifh *Rome*. Laftly, to fhew that no
power

power can rest upon a steep, hee must precipitately be forced to send Embassadors to *Rome* (with his Sword in his scabbard) servily begging mercy, and grace of such reconciled enemies, whose endlesse ends of spirituall, and temporall Supremacy (this Princesse knew) would never forgive any heavenly Truth, or earthly power that should oppose their Combination. Finally she concluded that hollow Church of *Rome* to be of such a *Bucephalus* nature, as no Monarch shall be ever able to bestride it, except onely the stirring *Alexanders* of time present, wherein the world is passing finely overshot in her own bow.

Wherefore to end, (as I began) with the case of *Essex*, was not this excellent Princesse therein a witnesse to herselfe, that she never chose, or cherished. Favourite, how worthy soever, to Monopolize over all the spirits, and businesse of her Kingdome; or to imprison the universall counsels of
                                        nature,

nature, and State, within the narrow-
nesse of a young fraile mans luftfull, or
unexperienced affections? Not thinking any one, especially a Subject, better
able to doe all then her felfe. Where
like a worthy head of a great body, fhe
left the Offices, and Officers of the
Crowne free to governe in their owne
Predicaments, according to her truft.
Referving appeales to her felfe, as a
Sea—mark to warn all Creatures under
her that fhee had ftill a creating, or
defacing power inherent in her Crown
and Perfon, above thofe fubalterne
places by which fhee did minifter univerfall juftice. And though her wifdom
was too deep to nurfe or fuffer faction
amongft thofe great Commanders, and
diftributers of Publique Rights: yet
was fhee as carefull not to permit any
Ariftocraticall cloud, or pillar, to fhew,
or fhadow forth any fuperftitious, or
falfe lights between her and her people.

C AP.

## CAP. XVI.

AGaine in her houſhold affaires ſhe kept the like equall hands ballancing the ſloth or ſumptuouſreſſe of her great Stewards, and white ſtaves, with the providence, and reſervedneſſe of a Lord Treaſurer, kept up the Tables for Servants, Sutors, and for honors ſake in her owne houſe ; not ſuffering publike places to be made particular farmes of private men, or the honor of her houſhold to be carried into theirs : And withall, by the ſame reverend Auditor, ſhee watched over the nimble Spirits, ſelfe-ſeeking or large handedneſſe of her active Secretaries ; examining their Intelligence, money, Packets, Bils of tranſportation, Propoſitions of State, which they offer'd up by their places, together with Sutes of other Natures, in her
wiſdom

wifdome ftill fevering the deep buti-
neffe from the fpecious but narrow
felfneffe of inferior Officers.

Befides, all thefe were examined by
reverend Magiftrates, who having bin
formerly iffuers of her Majefties Treafure in the Secretaries places, did now
worthily become Governours of her
Finances, as beft able to judge between
the felfneffe of place,or perfon, and the
reall neceffities of her State, and Kingdome. A fine art of Government by
well chofen Minifters fucceffively to
wall in her Exchequer from the vaft
expence of many things, efpecially
upon Forraigne Ambaffadors, which
(fhe knew) could neither bring reverence, nor thankfulneffe to their Soveraigne.

Under which head of Forraigne, and
Domeftique Ambaffadors, the anfwer
wherewith that Majefticall Lady entertained the *Polarke*, expected a treating
Ambaffador, but proving (as fhe told
him) a defying Herald, is never to be
P         forgotten

forgotten among Princes, as an inſtance how ſenſible they ought to be of indignity, and how ready to put off ſuch ſudden affronts, without a prompting of Councellors; againe worthily memorable among her Subjeƈts, as a demonſtrative argument that ſhe would ſtill reſerve *Moſes* place entire to her ſelfe amongſt all the diſtributions of *Iethro.*

And to go on with her Domeſtique affaires how provident was ſhe, out of the like caution, and to the ſame end, that even hee who overſaw the reſt, might have his owne greatneſſe overſeen, and limited too, VVhereupon ſhe forgot not to allay that vaſt power and juriſdiƈtion of her Treaſurers Office, with inferior Officers of her Finances, and perchance under an aƈtive Favourits eyes, kept her owne; Beſides ſhe watched and checked him in his marriage made with *Paulet* his Predeceſſor, reſerved that mans accounts, and arrears as a rod over his
Grandchilds

Grandchilds alliance, qualified, and
brought the fines of his many, and great
Copyholds to eafie rates, would never
fuffer any propofition to take hold of
uniting the Dutchy of *Lancafter* to her
Exchequer, what narrow reafons foever were alleaged of fparing and cutting off the multiplicity of Officers,
with their wages and ignorances or
corruptions, all chargable, and cloudy
paths, which the dealing with Princes
moneys doth as naturally bring forth,
as *Africa* doth Monfters. But like a
provident Soveraigne, knowing that
place in a Monarchy muft help as well
to traine up fervants, as to reward,
and encourage merit; fhe conftantly
(to that end) keeps that Chancellor-
fhip of the Dutchy entire, and will
not make the rewarding part of her
Kingdome leffe, to overload her Exchequer with any addition of inftru-
mentall gaine amongft under Officers,
into whofe barns thofe harvefts are in-
ned for the moft part.

P 2                 Again

Again with the fame caution in all her
doings fhe made merit precious, honour dainty,and her graces paffing rare,
keeping them (as the Venetians doe
their curioufly refined gold) to fet an
edge upon the induftry of man, and yet
(like branches of Creation) fparingly
referved within the circuit of her
Throne, as inherent, and tender Prerogatives, not fit to be left at randome in
the power of ambitious Favourites, or
low-looking Councellors, whofe ends
are feldome fo large,or fafe for the publique, as the native Princes Councels
are, or ought to be.

For her Clergy with their Ecclefiafticall, or Civill jurisdictions, fhe fafhioned the Arches, and Weftminfter
Hall to take fuch care one to bound
another, that they in limiting themfelves, enlarged their Royalties, as the
chiefe and equall foundations of both
their greatneffes ; fhe gave the fuperior
places freely, left by example fhe
fhould teach them to commit fy-
mony

mony with their interiors, and so adde
scandall in stead of reputation to Gods
Word, whose allowed Messengers they
affect to seem.

Her Parliaments she used, to supply
her necessarily expended treasure, and
withall, as Maps of orders, or disor-
ders, through her whole Kingdome. In
which reverent Body (as I said before)
she studied not to make parties, or
faction, advancing any present Royallist
in the nether House, to stir up envy upon her self amongst all the rest, and so
publish the Crowne to use personall
practises of hope, or feare, in these
generall Councels of her Kingdome,
but by forbearing art was never troubled with any artificiall brickwals from
them; so as their need and fears concurring with her occasions, made their de-
sires and counsels concurre too, and out
of those equall, and common grounds
forced every man to beleeve his private
fish ponds could not be safe, whiles the
publique state of the Kingdome stood

in

in danger of prefent, or expectant extremities.

Her Councell-board (as an abridgment of all other jurisdictions) she held up in due honour, propounded not her great businesses of State to them with any prejudicate refolution, which once discovered, supprelseth the freedome both of spirit and judgment, but opens her selfe clearly, heares them with respect; observes number, and reason, in their voices, and makes a quintessence of all their concords, or discords within her selfe, from whence the resolutions and directions came suddenly, and secretly forth for execution.

To be short, she kept awe stirring over all her Courts, and other imployments, as her antidote against any farther necessity of punishments; In which arts of men, and Government, her nature, education, and long experience, had made her become excellent above both Sexes.

Againe, for the Regiment of her Gran-

Grandees at home, she did not suffer the
Nobility to be servants one to another,
neither did her Gentry weare their Li-
veries as in the Ages before; their number and wealth was moderate, and their
spirits and powers counterpoiled with
her Majesty, from being Authors of
any new Barons Wars, and yet referved
as brave halfe paces between a Throne
and a people.

Her Yeomendry, a state under her
Nobles, and above her Peasants (proper
to England) she maintained in their
abilities, and never gave them cause to
suspect, she had any intent, with extraordinary Taxes out of the course of
Parliaments, insensibly to impoverish
& make Boors, or slaves of them, knowing that such a kind of champion countrey, would quickly stir up the Nobility it selfe, to become doubtfull of
their owne fences, and by consequence
in danger, not only of holding lives,
lands, goods, and Liberties at their Soveraignes indefinite pleasure, but by

suspence

suspence of those nursing, and protecting Parliaments, to have all other native birthrights, *viz*. Pulpits, Lawes,
Customes, Voyces of Appeale, Audits
of Trade, humble, and reverent mention
of Coronation-oaths; legall publishers,
and maintainers of War, true Maps of
Diseases, and cures through her Kingdome, with many other mutuall ci-
ments of honour, and use, between Soveraigne, and subjects, like to be con-
founded, or at least metamorphosed
into Prerogative Taxes, wherein the
people neither have voyces, nor valu-
able returne. I say, this home-borne
Princesse of ours making her prospect
over these wildernesses of will, and
power, providently for her selfe, and
happily for us, refused the broad branch
of *Pythagoras* Y, and chose that narrow-
er, but safer medium of State-assem-
blies, concluding that these two Honourable Houses, were the only judicious, faithfull, and industrious Favorites of unincroaching Monarchs.

So

So that it appears fhe did not affect, nor yet would be drawne (like many of her ancient Neighbours the French Kings) to have her fubjects give away their wealth after a new fafhion, *viz.* without returne of Pardons, eafe of grievances, or comfort of Lawes, left her loving people might thereby dream of fome fecret intent to indennize their lives, wealth, and freedomes, into a fhip of *Athens*, of which the name being old, and all riders, fleepers, and other Timbers new, they were to be fhipped downe a ftreame of the like nature ever, and yet never the fame. Befides not to be fhipped into that fhip as Mariners, Souldiers, Saylors, or Factors, but rather as flaves, or conquered Out-Laws, with great difhonour to the Legall, and Royall ftate of Monarchicall Government, as fhe conceived. From which example of chafte power, we that live after this excellent Lady, may with great honour to her afhes refolve, that fhe would have been as adverfe from

bearing

bearing the envy of printing any new
Lines of Taxe, Impofitions, Proclamations, or Mandats (without Parliaments) upon her ancient cœleftiall, or
terreftriall Globes, as her humble fubjects poffibly could be, or wifh her to
be.

Now if we fhall examine the reafon
of her cutting between Lawes, Kings
powers, and the Peoples freedome, by
fo even a thread, what can it be, but a
long and happy defcent within the pedegrees of active Princes, together with
the moderating education of Kings
children in thofe times; or laftly in a
quinteffence of abilities, gathered out
of thofe bleffed, and bleffing mixtures of
nature, Education, and Practice, which
never faile to lift up man above man,
and keep him there, more then place or
power fhall by any other encroaching
advantages ever be able to doe.

In which Map, as in a true perfpective glaffe, this provident Princeffe
feeing both her owne part, and her
peoples,

peoples, fo equally, nay advantagioufly
already divided, and difpofed, fhee
thought it both wifdome, and juftice to
leave them ballanced, and diftinguifhed
as fhe found them ; Concluding that
the leaft change of *Parallels*, or *Meridian*
Lines newly drawne upon any the ancient Globes of Monarchall Government in abfence of Parliaments, would
(like the fervice of God in an unknown
Language) prove prophaned, or mifun-
derftood ; And confequently regifter
fuch a Map of writing, and blotting
of irregular raifing, and depreffing dif-
advantagious matching of things reall,
and humours together, as muft multiply Atheifme in humane duties, caft
trouble upon her Eftate for want of
reverence at home, and provoke this
heavy cenfure through all the world
(*Spaine* only excepted) that fhe endeavoured the raifing of an invifible
Tyrant above the Monarch ; and to
that end had made this ftep over Lawes,
and Cuftomes into fuch a dangerous
kind

kind of ignorant, and wandring confusion, as would quickly enforce mankinde, either to live like exhausted
creatures, deprived of Sabbaths, or like
barren earth without priviledge of
any Jubile, which metamorphosing
prospect (as they thought) would re-
semble *Circes* guests, transforme her
people into divers shapes of beasts ;
wherin they must lose freedome, goods,
fortune, language, and kinde, all at
once.

An inchanted confusion imaged
by the Poets, to warne Princes, that if
they will easily be induced to use these
racks of wit, and power indefinitly, and
thereby force a free people into a des-
pairing estate, they must even in the
pride of their Governments, looke in
some sort to be forced againe, either to
sacrifice these *Empsons*, and *Dudleyes*,
as the most popular act such Princes
can doe, or else with the two edged
sword of Tyranny, irregularitie to
climbe a degree yet higher then the
truth,

truth, to maintaine thefe Caterpillars
in eating, or offering up Religion,
Lawes, &c. to the covetous, cruell, or
wanton exceffes of encroaching Tyranny, as though God had made all the
world for one.

Nay more it pleafed this provident
Queen even curioufly to forefee, what
face her eftate was like to carry, if thefe
biaced humours fhould continue any
long raigne over us, *viz.* contempt to
be caft over the Majefty of the Crown,
feare among the people, hate and envy
againft the reverend Magiftrate, en-
tifement of domeftique fpirits to mutiny, or forraigne to invade upon any
occafion, the Court it felfe becomming
a Farme, manured by drawing up, not
the fweet, but even the browes of humble fubjects; and laftly the Councell-
boord, that glorious type of Civill
Government, compelled to defcend, and
become Broker for money, executioner
of extremity, better acquainted with
the Merchant, or mechanicall fcraping
Revenues

Revenues of ficke, and exhaufted Kingdomes, then forraigne Treaties, equall
ballances of Trade, true grounds of
Manufactures, myfteries of Importa-
tion, and Exportation, differing
ftrengths, and weakneffes of Crownes,
alteration of Factions, or parties with
advantage, danger of alliances made to
the benefit of the ftronger, the fteady
(though fometimes intermittent) undertakings of the Conqueror, with all
things elfe that concerne *Magnalia
Regni*, and fo apt inftruments, not
reverently to fhew Princes the truth,
but rather felf-loving creatures full of
prefent and fervile flatteries, even to the
ruine of that Eftate wherein they have
and enjoy their honours.

Which confufion of place and things
being cleerly imaged within her, perfwaded this Lady to reftrain the flavifh
Liberties of Tranfcendency, within
Lawes, and Parliaments, as two un-
batter'd Rampires againft all over-
wreftings of power, or mutinies of
people,

people, and out of these grounds to
conclude Prince-like, with her fore-
fathers, that *superstructiones antiquæ nec
facile evertuntur, nec sole ruunt.* In this
axiome making manifest to the world,
that time presents children, with their
young, and unexperienced capacities,
are much too narrow moulds, for any
large branches of well-founded Monarchies to be altered, or new fashioned in,
the new and old seldome matching well
together, let the Ciment of seeming
wisdome on either side appeare never so
equall.

Now for the right use of these high
pillars, if we shall descend to inferior
functions, we there find her (like a wor-
king soule in a healthfull body) still,
all, in all, and all in every part. For
with the same restraining providence,
she kept the Crowne from necessity to
use Imperiall, and chargable Mandates
upon her people, when she had most
need of their service, contrary to the
wisdome of all Government ; Neither
did

did she by mistaking, or misapplying
instances (gathered out of the fatall
conquests of her Ancestors) parallell
her present need, and Levies with theirs,
but wisely considered that the King,
and the people were then equally pos-
sessors of both Kealmes, and so in all
impositions contributers to themselves
at the first hand.

From which grounds, like a conten-
ted and a contenting Soveraigne, she
acknowledged these differences to be
reall, and accordingly by an equall audit
taken from her itinerant Judges, with
the Justices inhabiting in every Coun-
ty, after she was well informed of her
subject, abilities, and her enemies
threatnings, she then, by advice of her
Privy-Councell summon'd her Parliaments, demanded ayd, and was never
refused; In returne of which loving and
free gifts, she disposed those extraordinary helps to the repayring, and pro-
visionall supplying of her Forts along
the Coast, with offensive and defensive
munitions,

munitions, fhe ftored her Office of the Ordnance as a royall Magazine to furnifh the whole Kingdom in extremity, and when there were no wars, yet fhe kept it full, as an equall pledge of ftrength, and reputation, both abroad, and at home.

Laftly, this Princeffe being confident in thefe native Sea-walls of ours, fit to beare moving Bulwarkes in martial times, and in Civill Traffiques to carry out, and in, all Commodities with advantage; fhe double ftored her Navy Magazines with all materials, provided before hand for fuch workes, and things, as required time, and could not be bought with money; befides, fhe furnifhed her Sea Arfinals with all kind of ftaple provifions, as Ordnance, Pitch, Rofin, Tar, Mafts, Deale boards, Cordage, &c. for the building, and maintaining of her Navie, flourifhing in multitude of Ships for War and Trade.

And as the life of that vaft body,

fhe

she for encreafe of Mariners, gave Princely countenance to all long voyages, knowing they would neceffarily require Ordnance, new munition, and burthen; and further to encourage this long-breathed worke, she added out of her Exchequer an allowance of fo much in the tun for the builders of any ships upward of fo many hundred Tuns; She cherifhed the fifher-boats with priviledges along her Coafts, as nurferies of Sea-men; brought *Groniland*, and *New-found-land* fifhing in repuration to encreafe her flock of Mariners, both by taking, and tranfportingwhat they took far off.

And for the Governours of her Navy under the Admirall, as well in times of peace as war, she chofe her principall Officers out of the gallanteft Sea Commanders of that time, whofe experience she knew taught them how to husband and guide her. *Mufcovy* Company in generall Provifions, not as partner with her Merchants in building,

ing, but reſtraining the Ship-keepers
riot, or expence in harbour, and at Sea,
how to furniſh, or martiall ſhips, and
Mariners in all kind of Sea-fights to
their beſt advantage.

Beſides, through the ſame mens judg-
ments, ſhe made all directions paſs for
the divers moulds required in ſhipping betweene our Seas, and the Ocean;
as the drawth of water, high, or low,
diſpoſing of ports, cleanly roomes for
Victuals, convenience of Deckes for
Fight, or Trade, ſafe conveyance for
Powder, & all other munition, fit Stow-
age of Sea ſtores, according to the difference of heats, or colds in the Climes
they were to reſide in, or paſſe through.

Againe, as well to inſtruct the Captaines in their particular duties, as to
keep a hand of Government over the
large truſt, and charge committed to
them, in all expeditions, the Ship with
her furniture, tackling, and men, the
Gunners Roome with all munition of
that kind, the Boat-ſwains proviſion of

An-

Anchors, Cables, Canvas, and Sea-
ſtores, the Purſers, Stewards, and
Cooks Roomes touching victuals were
delivered to the Captaines by Bill
indented; the one part kept with the
Officers of the Navy at home, the other
in the hands of every private Captaine
to examine his accounts by when he
return'd: of which my ſelfe am wit-
neſſe, as being well acquainted with the
uſe of it in my youth, but utterly un-
acquainted with the change ſince, or
any reaſons of it.

Laſtly, this great Governeſſe could
tell how to worke her high Admirals
(without noiſe) to reſign their Patents,
when the courſe of times made them
in power, and gaine, ſeeme, or grow
too exorbitant; yet kept ſhe up their
Command at Sea, and when they were
there made them a limited, or abſolute
Commiſſion under the great Seale of
*England*, ſometimes aſſociating, and
qualifying their place, with a Councell
of war of her own choice, and ever guiding

ing the generalities of the Voyage with inftructions proper to the bufinefs, and to be publifhed at Sea in a time prefixed.

Out of which caution in her principall expeditions, fhe ftriving (as I faid) to allay that vaft power of place with fome infenfible Counterpoife, many times joyned an active Favourite with that Sea *Neptune* of hers, making credit, place, and merit, finely competitors in her fervice; Befides, fhe well underftanding the humours of both, temper'd them fo equally one with another in her latter expeditions, as the Admirall being remiffe, and apt to forgive all things, *Effex* feverely true to Martiall Difcipline, and loath to wound it by forgiving petty errours under that implacable Tyrant *Mars*, in all likelihood her Fleet could hardly be over failed, or under ballafted, and confequently the Crowne (in her abfence) was fure to be guarded with more eyes than two, to prevent confu-

Q 3                fufion

fusion in Martiall Affaires, where every Ship proves beyond the amendment of second thoughts, and so fatall to that state which paies, and negligently ventures.

The Merchant-part of her Kingdome was oppressed with few impositions, the Companies free to choose their owne Officers, to fashion their Trade, assisted with the name and countenance of her Embass dors, the custome, and returne of their industry, and adventures, contenting them in a free Market without any nearer cutting of peoples industry to the quick.

The *Flushingers*, and *Dunkerkers* in succession of time, it is true, did much afflict their Traffique, though with smal strength; whereupon she first travelled to suppresse them by force, but found the Charge grow infinite, and the cure so casuall, as she joyned Treaty with the Sword, and set her Seas by that providence, and industry, once againe at liberty from all molestation, or danger of Pyrates.                     Her

Her Univerfities were troubled with
few *Mandates*, the *Colledges* free in all
their Elections, and governed by their
own Statutes, the groffe neglect of ufing
the Latine Tongue fhe ftudied to reforme, as well for honour of the Univerfities, as for her own fervice in all
Treaties with Forraign Princes, fhe
ftudied to multiply her *Civilians*
with little charge, and yet better allowance to their Profeffion.

In a word, fhe preferved her Religion without waving, kept both her Martiall, and Civill Goverment intire a-
bove neglect, or practice, by which,
with a multitude of like inftances, fhe
manifefted to the World, that the well
governing of Princes own Inheritan-
ces, is ( in the cleare houfe of Fame)
fuperiour to all the far noifed conquefts of her over-griping Anceftors,
fince what Man lives, converfant in the
*Calenders* of eftates, but muft know,
that had not thefe wind-blown conquefts of ours happily been fcattered,

they muſt in time have turned the moderate wealth, and degrees of *England* into the naſty poverty of the French peaſants ; brought home Mandates in ſtead of Lawes, waved our freedomes in Parliaments with new chriſtned Impoſitions, and in the end have ſubjected native and active *Albion* to become a Province, and ſo inferior to her owne dearly bought forraign conqueſts, being forced to yeeld up the ſuperlative works of power, to the equall Laws of Nature, which almoſt every where ( *America* excepted ) proclames the greater to be naturally a Law-giver over the leſſe.

*CAP.*

## CAP. XVII.

YEt as this wife and moderate Governeffe was far from incroaching
upon any other Princes Dominions, fo
wanted fhe neither forefight, courage
nor might, both to fuppreffe all info-
lencies attempted againft her felfe, and
to fupport her Neighbours unjuftly
oppreffed, whereof by the Readers pa-
tience I will here adde fome few inftances.

She had no fooner perfected her
Virgin triumph over that fanctified,
and invincible Navy, and by that loffe
publifhed the Spanifh ambition weakneffe, and malice to all Chriftendome,
fecured her owne eftate, revived the
Netherlands, confuted the Pope, turned
the caution of the Italian Princes the
right way, and amazed the world ; but
even then to purfue that victory, and
prevent

prevent her enemies ambition, which ſtill threatned the world with new Fleets; then (I ſay) did this active Lady conclude, with adviſe of her Councell, and applauſe of her Kingdome, to defend her ſelfe thenceforth by invading, and no more attend the Conquerors pleaſure at her owne doores.

Out of which reſolution ſhe firſt ſent forth the Earle of *Cumberland*, who attempted the ſurprize of *Porto Ricco*, accompliſhed it with honour, and ſo might have kept it, had not diſeaſe, and diſorder proved more dangerous enemies to him, then the great name, and ſmall force of the Spaniſh did.

Againe to prevent danger, not in the bud, but root, ſhe tooke upon her the protection of *Don Antonio* King of *Portugall*, ſent Sir *Iohn Norris*, and Sir *Francis Drake*, with a Royall Fleet, and eleven thouſand men to land, ſeconded with the fortune, and countenance of the Earle of *Eſſex*; they tooke the baſe Towne of the Groyne, and when they

had

had overthrowne all that came to fuccour it, and burnt the Countrey, then
marched they on to *Lisbone*, and in that
journey facked *Penicke*, wafted Villages,
and Provinces, entred the fuburbs of
*Lisbone* even to the gates of the High
Towne, and burnt threefcore Spanifh
hulkes full of provifions.

And to the fame end, fhe did, and
ftill meant fucceffively to maintaine a
Fleet of her owne Ships, and her faft
friends the Netherlands upon his
Coafts, not only to difturbe the returne
of victuals, munition, and materials for
War, with which the Empire, Poland,
and the Hanfe Townes did ufually, and
fatally (even to themfelves) furnifh this
growing Monarch, but withall to keep
his Navy which was riding, and building in many havens, from poffibility of
getting head in any one place to annoy
her; and thirdly to fet fuch a Taxe upon
the wafting home of his Indian Fleets,
as might (in fome meafure) qualifie that
fearfull abundance which elfe was like
enough

enough to fpread infection through the
foundeft Councels, and Councellors of
all his Neighbour-Princes.

In the meane time, the French King
*Henry* the third (heartned by her example, and fucceffe) did encounter the *Gui-
fards*, a ftrong Faction depending upon
*Spaine*. And when he was made away by
treafon, & the Leagues in Armes under
the Spaniards protection, then did the
Queen providently take opportunity
to change the Seat of her Warres, and
affifted *Henry* the fourth, the fucceeding
King, by the Earle of *Effex*, untill he
was able to fubfift by himfelfe, and till,
by her fupport he was ftrengthened,
both to overthrow the League, and become a fecond ballance againft the
great, and vaft defires of *Spain*.

Neither did fhe reft here, or give him
breath, but with a Fleet of one hundred
and fifty Sayle, and a ftrong Land-army,
fent the Earle of *Effex*, and the Admirall of *England* to invade *Spain* it felfe,
they tooke *Cales*, fpoiled his Fleet of
twenty

twenty Gallyes, and fifty nine Ships,
the riches whereof were valued at
twelve millions of Duckets. Immediately after, imployed she not the Earle
of *Essex* with a Fleet to the Islands? In
which Voyage he sacked *Villa Franca*,
tooke prizes to the value of foure hundred thousand Duckets at the least.

Now when this Spanish Invader
found himselfe thus well paid with his
owne coyne, and so forced to divert the
provoked hand of that famous Queen
held over him, by stirring up *Tirone* in
*Ireland*; to which end he sent money,
and Forces under *Don Iohn d' Aquila,*
even then that Lady, first by *Essex*, and
after by *Montioy*, overthrew the Irish,
and sent home the Spaniard well re-
compenced with losse, and dishonour
for assisting her Rebels.

By which and the like active cour-
ses of hers in successive, and successefull
undertakings, that provident Lady both
bore out the charge of all those expeditions, requited his Invasion, clip-
ped

ped the fearfull wings of this growing Monarch, and made his credit fwell through all the mony-banks of Europe, caufing withall as low an Ebbe of his treafure.

Againe by this imprifoning of the Lyon within his owne den, fhe did not only leffen his reputation (a chiefe ftrength of growing Monarchs) but difcovered fuch a light as perchance might have forced him in time, to dif-pute the Titles of his Ufurpations at home, and have given *Fortugall*, *Arra-gon*, and *Granoda* opportunity to plead their rights with *Caftile* in the Courts of *Mars*, if God had either lengthened the dayes of that worthy Lady who underftood him, or time not neglected her wifdome fo fuddenly, by exchang-ing that active, victorious, enriching, and ballancing courfe of her defenfive Wars, for an idle (I feare) deceiving fhadow of peace. In which whether we already languifh, or live impoverifhed, whilft he growes potent, and rich, by the

the fatall fecurity of all Chriftendome, they that fhall fucceed us, are like to feele, and judge freely.

Thus you fee how our famous *Iudith* difperfed the terrour of this *Holofernes*, like a cloud full of wind, and by a Princely wakefulneffe, preferved all thofe Soveraigne States that were in league with her, from the dangerous temptations of power, wealth, and practice, by which the growing Monarchs doe often intangle the inferior, but yet Soveraigne Princes. And amongft the reft, from that ufefull traffique of his Leiger Embaffadors, who trained up in the nimble exchange of Intelligence, grow to be of fuch a *Bucephalus* nature, fo like *Rome*, as I faid before, a body of fuch members, as the *Alexanders* of their time can only mannage, and make ufe of ; Inftance *Mendofa*, in whom fhe had long before difcovered, and difcredited all practifes of thofe fpecious imployments of Conquerers Agents.

Befides in honour of her be it fpoken,

ken, did not this mirrour of Justice, by restraining that naturall ambition of getting other Princes rights, within the naturall bounds of well-governing her owne, become a beame of such credit, as most of the Kings, or States then raigning, freely yeelded; both to weigh their owne interests within the scales of her judgment, and besides to assist her in bounding out the Imperiall Meeres of all Princes by the ancient precession of Right, and power.

Lastly, did she not purchase the like reputation even amongst the heathen, and by it destroy'd a nest, which this aspiring Monarch began to build in the Seraglio of *Constantinople*; For she thinking it no wisdome to look on, and see his Spanish pistols pierce into so high a mountaine of Forces, and dispose of them at his pleasure, providently opened the stronger Monarchs eyes to discover how craftily the weaker wrought his ends at the cost of all defective, or sleepy Princes about her.

Yet

Yet did not this Soveraigne Lady
intercept his defignes from under any
Goddeffe fhield (whom *Homer* makes
the Grecian Worthies fhoot, and hit)
but difplanted him by a gallant Factor
of her Merchants in a league of Traffique, and prevailed to make his Em-
baffador landed at *Ragufa,* houfed in
*Conftantinople,* and all under protection
of *Ferrat* chiefe Vifier, yet, and upon a
contract of thirty thoufand zecchins
already paid him, glad to returne, and
fhippe himfelfe away, with more expedition then he landed.

Befides which reputation given to
her name by the Grand Signior in this
particular, fhe generally got power to
keep this fearfull Standard of the halfe
Moon waving in fuch manner over all
the King of Spaines defignes, as he
durft move no where againft his Neigh-
bour-Chriftian-Princes, for feare of
being incompaffed within the horns of
the heathen Crefcent.

R

But

But thefe things fwell, and require a
more authenticall Hiftory, to continue
the memory of that wonder of Queens,
and women ; in honour of whofe facred
name, I have prefumed thus to digreffe,
and admonifh all Eftates by her example, how they may draw ufe, and honour, both from the dead, and the living,
the change of times having no power
over reall wifdomes, but infinite over
the fhadowes of craft, and humours of
petty States, which commonly follow
the greater Bodies, as they are unequally extended, or contracted about them.

Wherefore now to conclude thefe
Heroicall Enterprifes abroad, together
with the reformations of her State at
home, the refining of the Englifh Standard embafed by her fifter, the prefer-
vation of her Crown-Revenue intire,
her wifdome in the change of Lawes,
without change of dangers, the timely
and Princely help fhe gave to *Henry*
the fourth when he had nothing but
the

the Towne of *Diepe* left him, his credit,
and meanes being utterly exhaufted,
and fo that brave King ready, either
to take Sea, and efcape, or flye for
fuccour into *England*, her conftant
eftablifhment of Religion in *Ireland*,
driving the Spanifh Forces divers
times from thence, who were ma-
licioufly fent as well to ftirre up her
fubjects to rebell as to maintaine, and
fupport them in it, together with the
former recited particulars, howfoever
improperly difperfed, or bundled up
together, yet are in their natures of fo
rare a wifdome, as I beleeve they will
ftill be more and more admired, and
juftly in that excellent Princeffe, even
many Ages after her death.

Thus have I by the Readers pati-
ence, given that Ægyptian, and Roman
Tragedy a much more honourable fe-
pulture, then it could ever have deferved, efpecially in making their memories to attend upon my Soveraignes
herfe, without any other hope of being,

then to wait upon her life, and death,
as their Maker did, who hath ever fince
been dying to all thofe glories of Life
which he formerly enjoyed, under the
bleffed, and bleffing prefence of this un-
matchable Queen and woman.

Now if any man fhall demand why
I did not rather leave unto the world a
complete hiftory of her Life, then this
fhort memoriall in fuch fcatter'd, and
undifgefted minutes, let him receive
this anfwer from a dead man, becaufe I
am confident no flefh breathing (by
feeing what is done) fhall have occafion
of asking that queftion, whileft I am
living. Prefently after the death of my
moft gracious Queen, and Miftrefs, the
falfe fpirits, and apparitions of idle
griefe haunted me exceedingly, and
made all things feeme either greater,
or leffe then they were; fo that the farther I went, the more difcomfortable
I found thofe new refolutions of time,
to my decayed, and difproportioned
abilities; yet fearing to be curfed with
the

the Figg-tree, if I bore no fruit, I rouzed up my thoughts upon an ancient axiome of Wife men; *Si quicquid offendit, relinquimus citò* ; *inerti otio torpebit vita* ; and upon a fecond review of the world, called to mind the many duties I ought to that matchleffe Soveraigne of mine, with a refolution to write her life in this manner.

Firft, ferioufly to have begun with the uniting of the Red, and White Rofes, in the marriage of *Hen:* the feventh; In the like manner to have run over *Henry* the eighths time, untill his feverall rents in the Church, with a purpofe to have demurr'd more ferioufly upon the fudden change in his Sonne *Edward* the fixth, from fuperftition to the eftablifhment of Gods Ancient, Catholique, and Primitive Church ; thofe cobwebs of re-converfion in Queen *Maryes* dayes, I had no intent to meddle with, but only by pre-occupation to fhew, that Princes captived

R 3                    in

in Nature, can feldome keep any thing free in their Governments, but as foyles manured to bring forth ill weeds apace, muft live to fee Schifme arife in the Church, wearing out the reall branches of immortall truth, to weave in the thin leaves of mortall fuperftition, and to behold in the State all their faireft induftries fpring, and fade together, like Ferne-feed; Laftly, I intended with fuch fpirits, as Age had left me, to revive my felf in her memory, under whom I was bred.

Now in this courfe, becaufe I knew, that as the liberality of Kings did help to cover many errours, fo truth in a ftory would make good many other defeds in the writer. I adventured to move the Secretary, that I might have his favour to perufe all obfolete Records of the Councell cheft, from thofe times downe as near to thefe, as he in his wifdome fhould think fit; hee firft friendly required my end in it, which I

as

as freely delivered him, as I have now done to you.

Againſt her memory he, of all men, had no reaſon to keep a ſtrict hand, and where to beſtow a Queen *Elizabeths* ſervant with leſſe diſadvantage to him-ſelfe it ſeems readily appeared not ; ſo that my abrupt motion tooke hold of his preſent Counſell. For he liberally granted my requeſt, and appointed me that day three weeks to come for his warrant, which I did, and then found in ſhew a more familiar, and gracefull aſpect then before, he deſcending to queſtion me, why I would dreame out my time in writing a ſtory, being as like to riſe in this time as any man he knew; Then in a more ſerious, and friendly manner examining me, how I could cleerly deliver many things done in that time, which might perchance be con-ſtrued to the prejudice of this.

I ſhortly made anſwer, that I concei-ved an Hiſtorian was bound to tell no-

thing

thing but the truth, but to tell all truths were both juftly to wrong, and offend not only Princes, and States, but to blemifh, and ftir up againft himfelfe, the frailty and tendernefle, not only of particular men, but of many Families, with the fpirit of an *Athenian Timon*; And therefore fhewed my felfe fo far from being difcouraged with that objection, as I took upon me freely to adventure all my own goods in this Ship, which was to be of my owne building. Immediately this Noble Secretary, as it feems, moved, but not removed with thofe felfeneffes of my opinion, ferioufly affured me, that upon fecond thoughts he durft not prefume to let the Councell-cheft lie open to any man living, without his Majefties knowledge and approbation.

With this fuperfedeas I humbly took my leave, at the firft fight affuring my felfe this laft project of his would neceffarily require fheet after fheet to
be

be viewed, which I had no confidence
in my own powers to abide the hazard
of; and herein it may pleafe the Reader to beleeve me the rather by thefe
Pamphlets, which having flept out my
own time, if they happen to be feene
hereafter, fhall at their own perill rife
upon the ftage, when I am not; Befides, in the fame propofition I further
faw, that the many Judgements, which
thofe *Embryoes* of mine muft probably
have paft through, would have brought
forth fuch a world of alterations, as in
the end the worke it felfe would have
proved a ftory of other mens writing,
with my name only to put to it, and fo
a worfhip of time, not a voluntary homage of duty.

Farther I cannot juftifie thefe little
fparkes, unworthy of her, and unfit
for me; fo that I muft conclude with
this ingenuous *Confeffion*, that it grieves
me to know I fhall ( as far as this abrupt Apology extends ) live, and dye
up-

upon equall tearmes with a Queene,
and Creature fo many waies unequall,
nay, infinitely fuperiour to me, both
in Nature, and Fortune.

✿✿✿✿✿✿✿✿✿✿✿✿✿✿✿✿✿✿✿✿✿✿

## CAP. XVIII.

NOw to return to the Tragedies re-
maining, my purpofe in them was,
not (with the Ancient) to exemplifie
the difaftrous miferies of mans life,
where Order, Lawes, Doctrine, and
Authority are unable to protect Inno-
cency from the exorbitant wickedneffe
of power, and fo out of that melan-
cholike Vifion, ftir horrour, or murmur againft Divine Providence : nor
yet (with the Moderne ) to point out
Gods revenging afpect upon every
particular fin, to the defpaire, or confufion of mortality;but rather to trace
out the high waies of ambitious Governours,

vernours, and to fhew in the practice,
that the more audacity, advantage, and
good fucceffe fuch Soveraignties have,
the more they haften to their owne defolation and ruine.

So that to this abftract end, finding
all little inftruments in difcovery of
great bodies to be feldome without errours, I prefumed, or it rather efca-
ped me, to make my Images beyond
the ordinary ftature of exceffe, wherein again that women are predominant,
is not for malice, or ill talent to their
Sexe ; But as Poets figured the vertues
to be women, all Nations call them by
Feminine names, fo have I defcribed
malice, craft, and fuch like vices in the
perfons of Shrews, to fhew that many
of them are of that nature, even as we
are, I meane ftrong in weakneffe ; and
confequently in thefe Orbes of Paffion, the weaker Sexe, commonly the
moft predominant; yet as I have not
made all women good with *Euripides*,

fo

fo have 1 not made them all evill with *Sophocles*, but mixt of fuch forts as we find both them, and our felves.

Againe, for the Arguments of thefe Tragedies they be not naked, and cafuall, like the Greeke, and Latine, nor ( I confeffe ) contrived with the variety, and unexpected encounters of the Italians, but nearer Level'd to thofe humours, councels, and practices, wherein I thought fitter to hold the attention of the Reader, than in the ftrangenefs, or perplexednefs of witty Fictions ; In which the affections, or imagination, may perchance find exercife, and entertainment, but the memory and judgement no enriching at all; Befides, I conceived thefe delicate Images to be over-abundantly furnifhed in all Languages already.

And my Noble Friend had that dexterity, even with the dafhes of his pen to make the *Arcadian* Antiques beautifie the Margents of his works; yet the

honour

honour which ( I beare him record) he
never affected, I leave unto him, with
this addition, that his end in them was
not vanifhing pleafure alone, but morall Images, and Examples, ( as dire-
&ing threds ) to guide every man
through the confufed *Labyrinth* of his
own defires, and life : So that howfoever I liked them not too well (even in
that unperfe&ed fhape they were ) to
condefcend that fuch delicate (though
inferior ) Pi&ures of himfelfe, fhould
be fuppreffed; yet I do wifh that work
may be the laft in this kind, prefuming
no man that followes can ever reach,
much leffe go beyond that excellent
intended patterne of his.

For my own part, I found my creeping Genius more fixed upon the Images of Life, than the Images of Wit,
and therefore chofe not to write to
them on whofe foot the black Oxe had
not already trod, as the Proverbe is, but
to thofe only, that are weather-beaten

in

in the Sea of this World, such as having lost the sight of their Gardens, and groves, study to saile on a right course among Rocks, and quick-sands ; And if in this ordaining, and ordering matter, and forme together for the use of life, I have made those Tragedies, no Plaies for the Stage, be it known, it was no part of my purpose to write for them, against whom so many good, and great spirits have already written.

But he that will behold these Acts upon their true Stage, let him look on that Stage wherein himself is an Actor, even the state he lives in, and for every part he may perchance find a Player, and for every Line ( it may be ) an instance of life, beyond the Authors intention, or application, the vices of former Ages being so like to these of this Age, as it will be easie to find out some affinity, or resemblance between them, which whosoever readeth with this apprehension, will not perchance thinke
the

the Scenes too large, at leaſt the matter not to be exceeded in account of words.

Laſtly, for the Stile; as it is rich, or poore, according to the eſtate, and ability of the Writer, ſo the value of it ſhall be enhanſed, or cried downe, according to the grace, and the capacity of the Reader, from which common Fortune of Bookes, I look for no exemption.

But to conclude, as I began this worke, to entertaine, and inſtruct my ſe'fe, ſo if any other find entertainement, or profit by it, let him uſe it freely, judge honourably of my friend, and moderately of me, which is all the returne that out of this barren Stock can be deſired, or expected.

# FINIS.